Becoming a
LEGAL
MEDIATOR

Titles of Additional Interest

Becoming a Paralegal
Becoming a Police Officer
Becoming a Teacher
Paralegal Career Starter

Becoming a LEGAL MEDIATOR

New York

Copyright © 2010 Learning Express, LLC.

All rights reserved under International and Pan American Copyright Conventions.
Published in the United States by LearningExpress, LLC, New York.

Library of Congress Cataloging-in-Publication Data:
Becoming a legal mediator.—1st ed.
    p. cm.
  ISBN-13: 978-1-57685-761-8
  ISBN-10: 1-57685-761-1
  1. Mediation—United States. 2. Dispute resolution (Law)—United States. I. LearningExpress (Organization)
  KF9084 .B43   2010
  347 .73'9—dc22   2010020516

Printed in the United States of America

9 8 7 6 5 4 3 2 1

First Edition

ISBN-10 1-57685-761-1
ISBN-13 978-1-57685-761-8

For more information or to place an order, contact LearningExpress at:
  2 Rector Street
  26th Floor
  New York, NY 10006

Or visit us at:
  www.learnatest.com

About the Contributor

NORA EL ZOKM IS an aspiring attorney with a passion for public interest and peaceful conflict resolution. In her years as a paralegal for a Manhattan-based law firm, she prepared personal injury cases for mediation and facilitated their resolution. She is the founder of New York Legal Services, a service that drafts legal pleadings for New York attorneys.

Contents

Introduction: How to Use This Book   xi
      Step 1: Discover Legal Mediation   xii
      Step 2: Find Your Place   xii
      Step 3: Decide on Your Training   xiii
      Step 4: Conduct a Job Search   xiii
      Step 5: Succeed in Your New Profession   xiii

Chapter 1   **Legal Mediation 101**   1
      What Is Legal Mediation?   2
      The Stages of Legal Mediation   3
      Types of Cases Mediators Hear   7
      The Importance of Mediation   8
      What Legal Mediation Is Not   10
      Mediation, Arbitration, and Litigation Compared   11
      The Job Outlook for Legal Mediators   14
      Where Legal Mediators Work   15
      The Inside Track   20

CONTENTS

Chapter 2	**The History of Alternative Dispute Resolution**	**21**
	Alternative Dispute Resolution	21
	Timeline for ADR in the United States	23
	The Inside Track	30
Chapter 3	**Is Legal Mediation for You?**	**33**
	Motivations to Mediate	34
	Legal Mediator Suitability Test	37
	Personality Traits of the Successful Mediator	38
	Additional Qualities of the Legal Mediator	40
	Career Drawbacks	44
	What If Mediation Does Not Work?	46
	The Inside Track	48
Chapter 4	**Specialization within the Legal Mediation Field**	**49**
	Finding Your Niche	50
	Family Mediation	51
	Employer–Employee Mediation	56
	Landlord–Tenant Mediation	58
	Personal Injury Mediation	59
	Contract Mediation	60
	Mortgage Mediation	61
	Creating Your Niche	63
	The Inside Track	63
Chapter 5	**Credentialing and Training**	**65**
	Public Mediating Jobs	66
	Mediation Training 101	100
	The Inside Track	108
Chapter 6	**How to Find Your First Job**	**111**
	Internships and Practicums	112
	What Employers Look For	115
	Conducting Your Job Search	118
	Alternative Career Options	124
	The Inside Track	128

Chapter 7	**Job-Search Skills and Interviewing**	**129**
	What Your Resume Should Look Like	130
	Say It Clearly and Concisely	132
	Make Your Resume Computer Friendly	132
	What Goes on a Resume	136
	How to Tailor Your Resume	137
	Overall Content	139
	Addendum	152
	Writing a Cover Letter	152
	How to Format Your Cover Letter	153
	Write Clearly and Concisely	154
	What to Include in Your Cover Letter	154
	Surviving Your Interview	156
	Following Up on Your Interview	164
	The Inside Track	166
Chapter 8	**How to Succeed Once You Have Landed the Job**	**167**
	Joining a Group or Going It Alone	167
	Fitting into the Workplace Culture	168
	Managing Work Relationships	169
	Finding a Mentor	175
	Promoting Yourself	176
	Self-Employment	178
	Good Luck	185
	The Inside Track	186
Appendix A	**Professional Associations and Organizations**	**189**
	National Legal Mediation Organizations	189
	State-Specific Legal Mediation Organizations	191
Appendix B	**Legal Mediation Training Programs**	**199**
Appendix C	**Additional Resources**	**211**
	General Information	211
	Finding a Job	212
	Success on the Job	212
	Websites	212

CONTENTS

Appendix D	**Glossary of Legal Terms**	**215**
Appendix E	**Model Standards of Conduct for Mediators**	**219**
Appendix F	**Sample Rules of Mediation**	**227**
	1. Good Faith Effort	227
	2. Confidentiality	228
	3. Courtesy	228
	4. Role of the Mediator	228
	5. Representation	228
	6. Legal Counsel	229
	7. Termination of Mediation	229
	8. Arbitration and Court	229
	9. Exclusion of Liability	229

Introduction: How to Use This Book

Peace is not the absence of conflict but the presence of creative alternatives for responding to conflict—alternatives to passive or aggressive responses, alternatives to violence.
—Dorothy Thompson (1893–1961)

LEGAL MEDIATION is a growing field that shows no signs of slowing down. As other industries face economic troubles, mediation is becoming a more cost-effective way for businesses to resolve various disputes. Today, mediators are being used to handle disputes within many types of industries, including finance, mortgage, and banking. This trend, according to John Melamed of the American Institute of Mediation (AIM), is on an upward spiral.

Because mediators handle various types of disputes, a career in legal mediation presents an opportunity for individuals to enter a new field but still utilize their previous work experience, skill set, and educational background.

INTRODUCTION: HOW TO USE THIS BOOK

This guide contains an extensive discussion of how to go about becoming a legal mediator. As you read through each chapter, you will gain insight into the world of mediation, a type of alternative dispute resolution (ADR). This book will help you decide whether you have the qualities and traits to be a great mediator and what you can look forward to in this exciting career.

Think of this book as a road map: If you follow it, you will end up in an interesting and rewarding profession that is growing every year and shows no signs of slowing down. Here is a preview of some of the things you will see and do along the way.

STEP 1: DISCOVER LEGAL MEDIATION

Chapter 1 covers what legal mediation is and what a mediator does. You will read about the advantages of legal mediation over the traditional court system. In addition, you will discover the kind of salary you can expect as a mediator and the places where you might find employment.

In **Chapter 2**, you will learn the history of alternative dispute resolution (ADR). This is an umbrella term used to describe ways to resolve conflicts outside of litigation. You will see how alternative dispute resolution evolved into a legal movement, which provides a preferred way of addressing disputes over litigation within the court system.

STEP 2: FIND YOUR PLACE

Chapter 3 exposes the nuts and bolts of a mediator career. What personality traits make a great mediator? Is this job a good fit for you? This chapter demonstrates the qualities that make a solid legal mediator and describes both positive and negative aspects of the job.

Chapter 4 discusses how to find your niche within this field. One of the greatest things about being a mediator is that you have the opportunity to bring your previous experiences with you into your new career. In this chapter, you will read about the different areas of specialization and where your particular skill set would make you most valuable.

STEP 3: DECIDE ON YOUR TRAINING

Chapter 5 contains information about mediation credentialing and certification programs. Because this is a growing field, you want to make yourself as desirable as possible to potential employers. To that end, this chapter will discuss the different types of formal training you can obtain, where it is offered, and how much it costs.

STEP 4: CONDUCT A JOB SEARCH

In **Chapter 6**, you will find information about internships and apprenticeships, that will give you the opportunity to sit in on mediations and interviews with the opposing parties and even take part in the research leading up to the mediation. You will also find information on using other resources to help you find your first job and succeed in it.

Chapter 7 will show you how to write effective and attention-getting resumes and cover letters, and nail the scariest part of job hunting: the interview. Job hunting is rarely painless, but the hints in this chapter will ease your anxiety and allow you to come through the whole process intact and with a good job.

STEP 5: SUCCEED IN YOUR NEW PROFESSION

Finally, in **Chapter 8**, you will find advice that will help you succeed once you have found your job: how to be the best mediator you can be, how to build and maintain your client base, and how to build up your practice. It includes hazards to watch for in the workplace and how you can avoid them or recover from them. This chapter also shows you how to fit into your new job and get along with your colleagues and clients. And you will learn the importance of having a mentor and how to go about finding one, as well as other ways that you can promote yourself.

The appendices include lists of legal mediation associations and organizations and training programs, as well as additional book and website resources. There is also a glossary of legal terms you should become familiar with before embarking on your new career. Finally, you will learn about the *Model Standards of Conduct for Mediators*.

This book will tell you everything you need to know about becoming a legal mediator and will direct you to other resources as well. Whether you are just getting ready to graduate from high school or from college with a bachelor's degree, or you are in the workplace and want a change of career, or you are returning to work outside the home, the information in this book can help get you where you want to be. Good luck!

Becoming a
LEGAL
MEDIATOR

CHAPTER one

LEGAL MEDIATION 101

If you are considering a career in legal mediation, it is important that you understand exactly what legal mediation is and what a mediator does. In our lives, most of us have mediated a dispute for someone at some time—like the time you helped friends resolve a disagreement or worked with coworkers to bridge their various differences. In those cases, you essentially performed the functions of a mediator. Legal mediation, however, requires far more than sitting down with people and talking about their disputes.

A lean compromise is better than a fat lawsuit.
—George Herbert (1593–1633)

LEGAL MEDIATION is a meeting for resolving conflicts that involves a trained mediator as well as the parties having the dispute. This mediator does not favor either side of the dispute, but assists the parties in reaching a mutual resolution. The mediator is the central figure in this process, using his or her skills to establish cooperation between the parties and achieve the ultimate goal: both parties agreeing to a fair decision. Mediation has been used for a variety of conflicts, including commercial, legal, diplomatic, workplace, community, and family matters.

This may sound similar to the work of a judge or a lawyer. However, the mediator's approach is unique and makes this job vastly different from other conflict resolution professionals, such as arbitrators, judges, and lawyers. In contrast to a judge or a lawyer, the mediator does not decide who is right or wrong. He or she also does not necessarily apply the law to the dispute. Rather, the mediator works with the disputing parties—the individuals, corporations, or other legal entities involved in a conflict—so that they eventually agree on a solution to their conflict. The mediator's main goal is to facilitate the resolution of conflicts in a collaborative, mutually beneficial manner.

Another factor that makes legal mediation very different from other conflict resolution processes is that the mediator focuses more on the individual parties' values than on the law. The mediator will dedicate time to understanding clearly what is important to the parties and then use these factors to reach a resolution acceptable to both parties. These factors may include just about anything—morals, ethical values, ideologies, cultural factors, religious persuasions, or personal feelings about justice. This differs from other forms of conflict resolution, because it enables the disputing parties to decide what factors determine the outcome of their dispute.

WHAT IS LEGAL MEDIATION?

In her book *Alternative Dispute Resolution*, Jacqueline M. Nolan-Harley defines mediation as *a short-term, structured, task-oriented, participatory intervention process*. The term *participatory intervention* is extremely important. It emphasizes that mediation is a consensual process: it requires the mutual participation and agreement of *both* disputing parties.

Another very important part of legal mediation is the mediator, the impartial person who assists the two or more disputing parties in reaching their voluntary agreement. The objectivity of the mediator and the consensual nature of the process are earmarks of legal mediation.

Legal mediation approaches disputes from a fresh perspective. Instead of looking backward at who is to blame, it looks forward to what agreements the parties can reach to resolve their disputes.

The success of mediation rests largely on the willingness of the disputing parties to understand each other and to seek solutions that meet each other's needs. A legal mediator who feels that the parties are not willing to work toward this goal may decide that mediation is not appropriate for the particular dispute.

In legal mediation, the disputing parties are the decision makers, and the mediator's authority is limited. In other words, the disputing parties determine the issues that need to be addressed. The legal mediator helps the disputing parties understand each other's needs and interests to find common ground. From these, the disputing parties begin to generate solutions.

The solutions are not based on giving in, or compromising one's principles. Instead, they are based on a search for creative ways to resolve differences and meet identified needs. Agreements are reached only when the parties all agree. Because mediated agreements are voluntary, they are more likely to be honored by the disputing parties.

The legal mediator is always an active listener. He or she listens to what is being said attentively. The mediator's responsibility is not to give legal advice, even if he or she is a lawyer. The law is taken into consideration in the mediation process, but the individual values and concerns of the disputing parties are of utmost importance.

YOUR RESPONSIBILITIES DURING THE MEDIATION PROCESS

As a mediator, your responsibilities are

- to help parties identify the real issue at the heart of the dispute,
- to help parties distinguish between what they need and what they want,
- to help each party understand the other's issues and concerns, and
- to help both parties discuss and agree on a reasonable outcome to the dispute.

The legal mediation process is usually confidential. A good legal mediator ensures that the confidentiality of the disputing parties is maintained throughout the session.

THE STAGES OF LEGAL MEDIATION

A mediation session can be conducted in many different ways depending on the style of the mediator and what is most appropriate for the specific dispute. However, the process always includes an information exchange and a negotiation process between the two opposing parties.

The mediator will typically have both private and joint meetings between the opposing parties. In private meetings, the mediator meets with one of the disputants and perhaps his or her attorney. Joint meetings include both disputing parties. Often the mediator will decide upon the mediation format depending on the disputing parties and their relationship with each other. If there is a great deal of anger between the two parties, the mediator may decide to conduct the mediation in private meetings.

Typically, the legal mediation process includes the following steps:

1. **Preparing the process.** The mediator sets the stage with an introduction of all participants and words of encouragement. He or she discusses the ground rules and describes the process to the disputing parties.
2. **Sharing information.** The parties have an opportunity to share information and describe their desired outcomes. The mediator will request any outstanding and necessary documents that would be beneficial for the mediation. The mediator might also request the presence of experts or witnesses and their statements if he or she feels it is important for the case.
3. **Defining the issues and understanding interests.** The parties discuss the issues that need attention and the underlying needs and interests they hope to satisfy. The mediator decides whether this step is best accomplished in private or in joint meetings, depending on the level of hostility between the parties. In this step, the mediator takes a good look at the interests of the opposing parties and discusses the possible underlying positions they are maintaining within the dispute. The mediator also points out the emotional factors that may be contributing to a gridlock between the parties.
4. **Generating options toward a solution.** In this step, the mediator aids the parties in generating and evaluating options that will best suit their needs and interests. The mediator conveys how various options meet the disputants' needs and evaluates the proposed resolution options in light of the identified needs.
5. **Writing the agreement.** If a solution is reached and the parties desire a written agreement, the mediator may write or help the parties write an outline for agreed-upon future action. Once this agreement

has been drafted and signed, the final solution becomes binding. If one of the parties does not follow through on the terms of the agreement, they will be held responsible for their breach of contract.

The following example represents a sample written agreement for a case involving an employer–employee dispute. In this case, David Smith, an older male employee was placed on a Performance Improvement Plan by his significantly younger, newly hired female boss, Jane Jones. The reason for the placement on the Performance Improvement Plan, according to Ms. Jones, was because Mr. Smith was unable to use certain computer software that was vital for his job. He also refused to get training, stating that he had been able to do his job for many years without the software. Mr. Smith felt that the Performance Improvement Plan represented an attempt to get him fired and he was afraid of losing his job. He retaliated by filing a sex- and age-discrimination claim as he felt that his new supervisor was harassing him because he was an older male.

SAMPLE AGREEMENT

1. On November 4, 2002, David Smith and Jane Jones appeared for mediation. The terms outlined in this settlement agreement were the result of the mediation and were arrived at voluntarily.
2. Ms. Jones and Mr. Smith understand and agree that this settlement agreement does not constitute an admission of guilt, fault, or liability on the part of either party.
3. Mr. Smith agrees to withdraw his complaint of discrimination on the basis of sex and age, filed on October 1, 2002.
4. Ms. Jones agrees to withdraw the Performance Improvement Plan dated August 23, 2002.
5. Mr. Smith agrees to research and locate a course of training in Microsoft Office systems, which he will attend to completion. The date for completion will be no later than May 30, 2003.
6. Ms. Jones agrees to give Mr. Smith until May 30, 2003, to complete the course of training.
7. Ms. Jones agrees to grant the funding to cover the tuition costs and local travel costs incurred by Mr. Smith for the purposes of taking this course.

8. No later than two weeks after completing the course, Mr. Smith agrees to provide Ms. Jones with certification, provided by the trainer, of satisfactory completion of the course.
9. Ms. Jones agrees to accept the certification provided by the trainer as evidence of satisfactory completion of the course.
10. Both parties specifically acknowledge that Mr. Smith has preserved the following rights and responsibilities through the execution of this agreement:
    a. Mr. Smith has thoroughly reviewed and understood all the terms of this agreement.
    b. Prior to accepting and signing this agreement, Mr. Smith was informed of his right to consult with an attorney.
    c. Mr. Smith has had a period of twenty-one days in which to consider this agreement.
    d. This agreement will become effective and enforceable in eight days. Mr. Smith may revoke the agreement until then.
11. If either party herein fails to adhere to this agreement, or if a dispute arises out of or relating to this agreement, the parties agree to submit the matter to mediation prior to reinstating the complaint.
12. Both parties agree that this agreement represents the agreement in its entirety and that there are no other terms to this agreement except those specified herein. They further agree that this agreement may only be modified in writing and upon acceptance of all parties herein.
13. Both parties agree not to subpoena the mediator herein, nor any documents prepared by or for the mediator. Both parties also agree not to request the mediator to testify on their behalf in any way or for any reason, whether in person or in writing.

_____

David Smith   Date _____

Jane Jones   Date _____

Mediator   Date _____

THE PRINCIPLE OF SELF-DETERMINATION

At the heart of the mediation process lies the idea of self-determination, the belief that individual parties are ultimately responsible for resolving their dispute. The mediator is committed to helping people solve their disputes without pitting them against one another, which is different from what happens in a lawsuit. In order to uphold the integrity of the process, a mediator must believe that the disputing parties are capable and willing to decide the outcome of their conflict.

TYPES OF CASES MEDIATORS HEAR

One of the most appealing aspects of the mediation industry is its flexibility. The mediation process is applicable to most types of disputes and has been used, successfully, to resolve many civil (noncriminal) cases. In fact, mediation may even be applicable at times when litigation is not.

Mediation is most often used to resolve disputes between people. Mediation focuses on the underlying factors that are straining personal relationships and may be causing a barrier to conflict resolution.

Today, it is common for divorcing couples to use mediation when agreeing to the terms of a divorce. When a divorcing couple has children, the mediator will attempt to resolve the conflict in a way that salvages the relationship, enabling the couple to make joint parenting decisions in the future.

A mediator's skills are especially useful when approaching the topic of finance, alimony, maintenance, and child support. The mediator can help a divorcing couple come to an acceptable agreement about what is reasonable in the redistribution of funds.

A good family mediator will create a safe space, allowing the disputants to share financial information and assess their financial situation frankly. Instead of a court-ordered remedy to the conflict, a divorcing couple can design their own agreement, making it much more likely that they will abide by it.

It has become commonplace to use mediation to resolve workplace conflicts. Mediators hear cases that deal with wrongful termination, sexual harassment, and discrimination cases, in which there are invariably several perspectives to take into account. In such cases, mediations are successful because instead of focusing on who did what or who was wronged, the mediator focuses on getting both sides to acknowledge the other's perspective. Once that has occurred, the parties can commit to altering their behavior to respect each other's boundaries.

Mediators sometimes have a niche within educational institutions where they hear cases that can involve administrators, educators, students, and parents. These disputes are most often disagreements between administrators and educators regarding rules and regulations, curriculum changes, testing, and grading. Mediators also resolve conflicts between students or their parents or guardians and educators. For instance, at the university level, a mediator might hear sexual harassment allegation cases involving students and college professors. Mediators can be especially helpful in these situations because they protect the privacy of all parties involved. A confidential agreement is usually created to ensure that the student's boundaries are respected without the added stress of a public, formal hearing.

Another type of case that mediators hear involves disputes between business partners. Business partners have a vested interest in ensuring that their professional and personal relationship remains intact, and mediation facilitates this. These types of disputes often involve business decisions, work assignments, management styles, and employee relations.

Today, mediators are being used more and more frequently to hear commercial cases that, in the past, would have fallen solely under the jurisdiction of the court system. Commercial cases include personal injury cases (where an injured party and an insurance company come to some monetary agreement), landlord–tenant matters, contractual agreement issues, as well as professional negligence claims.

THE IMPORTANCE OF MEDIATION

Mediation is rapidly becoming an important and valued area within conflict resolution for several reasons.

Mediation represents a much cheaper way than litigation to resolve disputes. Most of us would agree that justice should be affordable and accessible to the masses. However, the reality is that lawyers are expensive. In addition, the litigation process can be drawn out and represent a serious financial burden for those seeking justice. Mediation is a way to relieve some of the financial issues associated with litigation. In litigation, an attorney for each party is present, whereas in mediation no attorney is required, although one may be used as a legal expert for both parties as opposed to representing only one party. In mediation, the length of time it takes to resolve the dispute is up to the disputants. If the matter is resolved within a few sessions, the cost will be minimal. In litigation, the amount of time it takes to resolve a dispute is in the hands of the courts and is often prolonged due to lengthy negotiations and court formalities. Mediation does not require court fees or hours of waiting for a judge to hear a case while an attorney is racking up an hourly rate.

Second, the notion of a speedy trial has become far more myth than reality in modern-day society, as James Melamed points out in his article, "A View of Mediation in the Future." There is a serious backlog of cases waiting to be heard in the court system. In fact, Melamed points out, statistics show that only 1.2% of cases filed in court are actually heard by a judge or jury. One main reason for this is that people simply get tired of waiting for their dramatic day in court. It gets too expensive, too emotionally draining, and too exhausting to wait for justice. Often, settlements are made out of sheer exhaustion and impatience, and not necessarily because a common agreement has been reached. The large volume of cases filed in court leads one to ask: Is it necessary to sue in the first place? The common conception is that the filing of lawsuits is necessary in order to get the attention of the other side. Although it may be true that the threat of a lawsuit motivates the opponent to pay attention, it is important to consider whether this is good use of the court's time.

The mediation process represents an entirely different approach. If mediation were the socially accepted mode of conflict resolution, what would that mean for our society? Perhaps it would mean that people had access to a fair agreement, which they themselves had created. People would be able to have their conflicts resolved in a timely fashion and would not be deterred from reaching out for help for financial reasons. Most importantly, mediation would offer the chance for the disputing parties to be in control and to have a say in the decisions that affect their lives. In mediation, nothing can be imposed on disputing parties, and the main focus is on compromise, concession, and agreement.

DOES MEDIATION REALLY SAVE TIME AND MONEY?

Going to court will absolutely settle your case. However, it will also be time consuming and costly, not to mention emotionally draining. Attorney fees may rise well above the estimated rate as the time to reach a decision in the congested courts takes months and even years.

In an attempt to identify just how much time and money is saved in mediation, the State of California conducted a study of five court-operated mediation programs between 2002 and 2003. In all five programs, the attorneys whose cases were resolved in mediation estimated that their clients saved approximately 61% to 68% in costs and 57% to 62% in billable hours. Counting all the savings together, disputants across all five programs saved a total of $49,409,385 and 250,220 hours. Not only is this excellent news for the public but it also frees up valuable court time, allowing judges to focus their energy on cases that are not appropriate for mediation.

WHAT LEGAL MEDIATION IS NOT

Litigation

Litigation is the process of taking a case through court, most commonly used for civil lawsuits. In litigation, there is a plaintiff (one who brings the charge) and a defendant (one against whom the charge is brought). In litigation, a judge or jury determines the dispute's outcome, with strict adherence to the law.

Professor Jack Ethridge of Emory University Law School explains drawbacks to this process: "Litigation paralyzes people. It makes them enemies. It pits them not only against one another, but against the other's employed combatant. Often disputants lose control of the situation, finding themselves virtually powerless. They attach allegiance to their lawyer rather than to the fading recollection of a perhaps once worthwhile relationship."

Arbitration

Arbitration is often considered a middle ground between litigation and mediation. In arbitration, the disputing parties present evidence to an arbitrator, who imposes a verdict on the parties. The arbitrator's function is very similar to that of a judge.

Counseling or Therapy

Good mediators can make the mediation process feel therapeutic for the disputing parties through their impartiality and active listening skills. However, the ultimate goal of the process is to resolve the dispute at hand, not the feelings of hurt or anger associated with the dispute.

MEDIATION, ARBITRATION, AND LITIGATION COMPARED

Mediation, arbitration, and litigation all share a common function: they are all forms of conflict resolution. However, there are vast differences among the three processes. Each process has its strengths and weaknesses. None of them should be approached as a one-size-fits-all method for resolving any type of dispute. As you consider a career in mediation, it is important that you understand exactly what differentiates it from other conflict resolution processes.

Litigation is the most commonly used process to resolve disputes. Litigation involves disputants appealing to the court system for conflict resolution. Mediation and arbitration, on the other hand, fall under the umbrella term *alternative dispute resolution* (ADR). These processes seek to resolve disputes outside of the court system.

One of the most important differences among the three processes is who gets to decide the outcome of the case. In litigation, a judge or a jury ultimately decides who wins and who loses. Typically, attorneys present their respective sides, following a set of rituals and rules that most laymen do not have access to. After hearing the attorneys' statements, a judge or a jury decides the fate of the disputants. In arbitration, the arbitrator or a group of arbitrators is the ultimate decision maker. One major difference between litigation and arbitration is that in arbitration, the parties decide in advance whether or not the decision is final. In litigation, the decision made by the judge or the jury is automatically final, although the decision can be reversed through a new, and lengthy, court process called an *appeal*. In this regard, mediation is vastly different. The disputants are the ones who decide the final outcome of their case. If they feel they are unable to reach a voluntary agreement, they may decide that mediation is not for them. In addition, the mediator does not have the authority to decide the outcome of the case for the disputants.

Among mediation, arbitration, and litigation, there are vast differences in the level of formality, the importance of rules, and the adherence to ritualized structures. Litigation is a highly formal process in which attorneys present arguments, argue legal statutes, and examine and cross-examine evidence. Every step in the process proceeds according to the customary guidelines. Deviation from these guidelines might lead to objections. In certain circumstances, deviation from the guidelines may result in a mistrial or for the verdict (the decision passed by the judge or the jury) to be overturned. One example of the formal structure of litigation has to do with the way in which evidence is presented. Attorneys have rules of evidence to follow when attempting to have this evidence admitted as part of their case. Although rules of evidence may seem like unnecessary legal technicalities, they serve as a way to ensure that the admitted evidence is fair to both parties.

RULES OF EVIDENCE IN LITIGATION

HEARSAY

Jane testifies that John has stated that Margaret is going on vacation. This is not evidence that Margaret went on vacation; Jane did not actually hear this information from Margaret. It is only evidence that John told her that. This kind of evidence is called *hearsay* and is usually not admissible in court.

PRIVILEGED INFORMATION

Information from healthcare providers, religious authorities, and between spouses is protected against disclosure. This kind of evidence is called *privileged information* and is typically not admissible.

The arbitration process is significantly less formal than the litigation process. An arbitration is similar to a private hearing with relaxed rules and regulations. The difference in formality can be seen clearly in the way in which evidence is introduced. An arbitrator does not have to abide by the rules of evidence. The arbitrator decides what evidence is admissible based on whether he or she deems it relevant to the case.

RULES OF EVIDENCE IN ARBITRATION

Rule 28 of the American Arbitration Association's Labor Arbitration states:

"The arbitrator shall be the judge of the relevance and materiality of the evidence offered and conformity to legal rules of evidence shall not be necessary."

Mediation is the least formal of the three processes. The mediator's function is to enhance the future relationship of the disputing parties, so the process is less adversarial than litigation or arbitration. In mediation, the formal court procedures do not apply and there are no rules of evidence.

Another important difference among mediation, arbitration, and litigation involves time and costs. Litigations often take years to resolve. The disputants must rely on the court schedules in order to get their cases heard. It is not uncommon for cases to take months or even several years to settle. There are significant court costs to pay in association with litigation. Also, because an attorney is necessary for the duration of the process, disputants are often left with expensive attorney costs. In arbitration, there are no court costs to pay. However, there are still arbitrator and attorney fees. Because the time it takes to resolve an arbitration case can be much shorter than litigation, the attorney costs are lower. Of the three processes, though, mediation is by far the cheapest and least time consuming. There are no court fees. Because it is a nonadversarial process, attorneys are not required, which eliminates attorney fees. In addition, if the disputants are willing to work together, their dispute can be resolved in a very short amount of time.

Next, when comparing mediation, arbitration, and litigation, it is important to keep in mind that litigation is a public event. Litigation proceedings are typically open to the public and records kept in association with litigations are publicly accessible. Both arbitrations and mediations are private. The agreements drafted during either process are kept off the record. Also, both mediators and arbitrators are required to keep the details of the proceeding confidential.

The three processes also differ in their basic approach to conflict resolution. Litigations and arbitrations are inherently adversarial processes, where the final decision is made by a third party based on his or her perception of what is relevant or important. At the heart of the mediation process, however, lies the idea that the disputing parties come to a voluntary agreement on their own, facilitated by the neutral third party. This often requires great effort from both the disputants and the mediator. However, if the agreement is entered into voluntarily, there is a greater chance that the disputants will abide by it. In litigation and arbitration, the agreement or decision is made by the third party. Thus, there may be residual discontent on the side of the losing party, making that party more likely to default on the terms of the agreement or appeal to have the agreement changed.

Another important difference among the three processes is the method used in bargaining and the effect that it has on the process and the disputants. In litigation, the opposing sides usually have a great deal of anger toward one another—a situation that the process does not help resolve. The process focuses on the past events. After hard bargaining by attorneys from both sides, the third party makes a decision in which one disputant wins while the other loses. This can be an emotionally draining experience for both parties. The arbitration process is also adversarial in nature. It, too, involves hard bargaining negotiation and concludes with one loss and one win. Mediations are the least emotionally taxing of the three processes. Here, the focus is not on past events, but on the disputants' future ability to communicate effectively. The method of negotiation in mediation focuses on compromise. Mediation requires that each party be able to cooperate with the other. It seeks to resolve the dispute by crafting an agreement whereby both parties win.

THE JOB OUTLOOK FOR LEGAL MEDIATORS

According to *U.S. News and World Report*, employment in arbitration, mediation, and conciliation *is expected to expand by 1,400 jobs, or 14 percent, between 2008 and 2018*, which is an above-average expansion rate for any industry. In fact, this report has included mediation in its top list of careers for several years. In 2008, a career in mediation was associated with high job satisfaction, little training difficulties, and average pay and degree requirements.

Another fact to keep in mind is that many individuals and businesses acknowledge the benefits to mediating, such as lower cost, shorter time, and confidentiality. As a result, mediation and other forms of alternative dispute resolution are often favored over litigation, leading to an increased need for ADR professionals. In fact, according to the Bureau of Labor Statistics, employment of arbitrators, mediators, and conciliators is expected to grow faster than the average (defined as an increase of 14% to 19% per year) through 2018. Today, most case types can be heard by an ADR professional. It has become more commonplace for mediators and arbitrators to be used in contract disputes, labor disputes, and other types of cases that in the past have been solely within the court's jurisdiction. Some types of cases, such as divorce and child custody, even require disputants to meet with a mediator.

Working as a mediator offers a good salary and some excellent benefits. According to the U.S. Department of Labor's Bureau of Labor Statistics, mediators can expect to earn between $28,090 and $102,202 per year, with median annual salaries estimated at $50,660. Hourly rates range from $13.50 to $49.05, with a median hourly wage of approximately $23.80.

WHERE LEGAL MEDIATORS WORK

Mediators work in a variety of environments. Mediators can be employed by the state or local government, the court system, schools and universities, or legal service providers (insurance carriers, corporations, private mediation groups, and private practices).

One of the greatest benefits to working as a mediator is that you can take your prior work experience with you. So, for example, if you come from a career in education, you might find mediating family matters cases to be a great way to use what you already know. The niche or specialization you choose will determine, to a great extent, where you will end up working. The following chart outlines where in the mediation field you might specialize based on your existing background, and shows you where you might find work based your mediation specialization.

Becoming a LEGAL MEDIATOR

Employment Venue	Case Type	Mediator Background
within the court system	contract disputes, personal injury, divorce, minor criminal infractions	law, social work, criminal justice, psychology
state and local government	employment discrimination, wrongful termination, taxation, securities	law, labor relations, securities, human resources
private dispute resolution groups	business contracts, personal injury, construction, employment	law, business, human resources, accounting, psychology
independent mediation	divorce, personal injury, employment, real estate, religious and ethnic, family, business, construction, discrimination	law, business, human resources, social work, parenting, psychology, education

MUST YOU BE A LAWYER TO BE A MEDIATOR?

Lawyers are legal experts; they are trained to be familiar with formal, written legal rules, known as statutes, and how those rules apply to various situations. It might seem that a law degree would serve as a good foundation for mediators. However, a law degree might not be the most useful degree for a mediator to have. It takes an entirely different skill set to be a good mediator. The rules of the law are far less important in mediation than understanding the dynamics between disputing parties. Although some kind of training or education would most likely benefit an aspiring mediator, law school is not necessarily the way to go. A report issued by the Society of Professionals in Dispute Resolution's (SPIDR) Commission on Qualifications stated that, "knowledge acquired in obtaining various degrees can be useful in the practice of dispute resolution."

In some instances, attorney-mediators may actually hinder the mediation process more than help it. Lawyers and mediators have a very different understanding of conflicts, and their processes for resolving them vary vastly. Mediations that are led by attorneys may end up resembling litigation with the attorney taking the lead, instead of helping the parties define their own issues.

In his article "Should a Mediator Also Be an Attorney?" mediator Chris Currie points out that the focus of an attorney-mediator tends to be on the facts of the case and the legalities involved. Currie concludes that "when attorney-mediators emphasize clarifying the facts at the expense of the relationship and communication issues, they may be inclined to see their subject-matter expertise as the key to settlement. When this happens, creative, more complete resolutions are frequently missed."

Currie also points out that legal education may desensitize lawyers to the emotional aspects and underlying issues of their clients' disputes. Legal reasoning causes law school students to look at the facts and how they apply to the law, sans the emotional content. This approach is useful in a court of law, but it is quite inappropriate in mediation, where the focus should be on understanding the hidden agendas of the disputants and helping them come to an agreement.

Another issue with attorney-mediators involves an attorney's method for resolving disputes. Lawyers are trained in conflict resolution via an adversarial approach. It can be very difficult, though not impossible, for them to apply a more collaborative approach to the resolution of their clients' disputes.

Self-Employment

Mediation offers an excellent opportunity for self-employment. Independent mediators in private practice handle their own paperwork and set fees and schedules. If you enjoy a large degree of autonomy and are interested in self-marketing, this might be a great option for you. Many people seek out independent mediators because the price is often lower than what they would pay for a mediator within a group.

Independent mediators often specialize in divorce and family mediation. It is customary for couples seeking a divorce to use a mediator, so there is a great deal of work available. For the mediator who is attempting to be self-employed, this specialization provides a possible steady stream of cases.

Private Dispute Resolution Groups

Many mediators join a private dispute resolution group or conglomerate. Most mediators are not directly employed by the dispute resolution group, but rather they sit on a panel and work as private contractors for the group. There are many advantages to being on a panel of mediators associated with a group. Typically, groups have administrative staff to handle paperwork and other tasks, take care of all advertising and marketing needs, and have contacts with insurance companies, attorneys, and other avenues to guarantee a steady stream of work. Most mediation groups insist that their mediators take training or certification courses, and often the group creates its own curriculum. Retired judges and attorneys frequently sit on mediation group panels. Some of the larger dispute resolution groups include the American Arbitration Association (AAA), the Academy of Family Mediators (AFM), Nassau Arbitration and Mediation, and the International Negotiation Academy (INA).

Mediation in the Court System

Some court systems (and almost every federal court of appeals) have a small number of mediators on staff to mediate various disputes for the courts. This practice has become a necessity for many court systems in order to decrease their operating costs and to lower the very heavy caseload that is bottle-necking the courts. Different states have different ways of doing this. Some mandate that people who file lawsuits meet with a mediator before they are able to proceed with the suit, others simply suggest it. Some courts make a conference room and a mediator available for disputes while others ask that people locate, and pay for, a mediator of their choice.

Mediation in the court system has been used to handle just about every type of civil matter possible, from contractual and business matters to personal injury to discrimination issues. In the family courts, mediation is widely used and has been instrumental in alleviating the court caseload.

That being said, there are some difficulties facing courtroom mediation. Due to a lack of public funding, courts often rely on inadequately trained volunteer mediators. Mediation programs also are often the first to be disposed of when public funding is cut. Until the mediation process is a more widely accepted method of conflict resolution, it will continue to be disposable as funds become limited.

Another problem facing courtroom mediation is maintaining the flexibility and informality of the mediation process within the rigid structure of the courthouse. In order for the mediation process to be successful, the informality of its structure is vital. Courts, however, do not function that way, so it can be a challenge to work the two systems simultaneously.

The good news is that in the instances where it has been used to handle federal or state disputes, mediation has seen some significant successes, including large class actions and mass torts. For example, a mediation process was able to resolve a nationwide class action brought in 1997 on behalf of African American farmers against the U.S. Department of Agriculture for racial discrimination. The settlement resulted in almost a billion dollars of benefits going to 22,000 farmers. Also, mediation has resolved major class action employment discrimination cases for major financial service firms, and in the automobile and retail industries. Finally, mediators have been involved in settling both the individual and large-scale disputes that resulted from the massive destruction caused by hurricanes in Florida, Louisiana, Alabama, and Mississippi.

One of the biggest advantages of using mediation in a courtroom setting is the scalability of the mediation process—meaning a mediation session can take thirty minutes, three hours, or three days—however long is needed to reach an agreement. In contrast, courts must uphold certain legal standards in order to fulfill their constitutional obligation to be fair (this is known as the court's *due process* requirement). Mediation processes are able to be effective without the lengthy and time-consuming due process requirements by which courts must abide.

Courts and due process agencies understand that they have a real need for mediation and other assisted voluntary settlement processes to manage their caseload. If more cases can be settled through mediation earlier in the process and at the lowest cost possible, then everybody wins! Mediation ultimately allows courts and agencies to take the necessary time and to deliver due process to those cases that need it most.

Becoming a LEGAL MEDIATOR

THE INSIDE TRACK

HON. JOHN P. DIBLASI (RETIRED)
JUSTICE OF THE SUPREME COURT, WESTCHESTER
NATIONAL ARBITRATION AND MEDIATION (NAM)

All of the mediators I work with here at NAM have a legal background. They were either lawyers or judges. This is helpful because as an attorney you are trained to understand both sides of the case and you have some understanding of what a likely jury outcome might be. Also, the attorneys who request me here at NAM, mostly do so with the knowledge that I was once a Supreme Court justice, so I can give the parties some information about what a likely decision might be depending on what jurisdiction their case is in.

But, there are also times where having been an attorney or judge hurts me. I always say that the best judge-mediators are the ones that can forget to be a judge. As a lawyer you have certain preconceived notions, certain biases and cynicisms that don't apply in mediation. In mediation, I am not operating as a judge or an advocate. I have to actively remind myself to back off from the process and just allow the parties to vent. If the invitation is extended to me, then I can maybe offer some suggestions, I might use some of my knowledge as a judge to explain to them what might happen in court or what problems they might incur. But it can be difficult to remember. It also can be difficult when the attorneys know my background and look to me to decide the case, to function as a judge when I really can't.

CHAPTER two

THE HISTORY OF ALTERNATIVE DISPUTE RESOLUTION

In the United States, the process of legal mediation was developed as a response to the public's dissatisfaction with the available forms of conflict resolution. However, other forms of conflict resolution were used long before mediation was adopted in the United States.

The courts of this country should not be the places where resolution of disputes begins. They should be the places where the disputes end after alternative methods of resolving disputes have been considered and tried.
—Justice Sandra Day O'Connor (1930–)

ALTERNATIVE DISPUTE RESOLUTION

Mediation falls under the larger category of ADR. This umbrella term refers to various forms of dispute resolution that do not involve litigation, such as mediation, arbitration, and negotiation. In the United States, ADR was seen as a law reform movement beginning in the 1970s when people began to take issue with the negative effects of litigation. As legislation in the 1960s continued to grant more and more individual rights, a need developed for an effective way for people to seek legal recourse when these rights were infringed upon. It did not take long for the courts to experience docket congestion and for legal costs and wait time to increase. A need for an alternative to litigation was born.

In 1976, Chief Justice Warren Burger convened the Roscoe E. Pound Conference on the Causes of Popular Dissatisfaction with the Administration of Justice (or Pound Conference) in Minneapolis, Minnesota. Here, many members of the legal profession came together in an attempt to find some new method to deal with legal disputes. At the conference, Harvard Law School professor Frank Sander presented his paper "Varieties of Dispute Resolution," which formed the basic understanding of ADR. "Varieties of Dispute Resolution" proposed that the legal community begin to look at the processes by which various legal decisions are made and match individual legal conflicts with the most appropriate form of redress: mediation, arbitration, and the like. In his paper, Sander also proposed a multi-door courthouse, and this idea was adopted in Houston, Texas, in Tulsa, Oklahoma, and in the District of Columbia. "Varieties of Dispute Resolution" turned Sander into a pioneer for the field of ADR.

> Eastern cultures use mediation more commonly than they use the formal court system. In China, for example, disputes are resolved through mediation approximately 35 times more often than through the courts.

Today, ADR has become a widely accepted form of conflict resolution. It has woven its way into the fabric of state and federal court proceedings, and courses on ADR are being taught in law schools across the country.

MEDIATION IN ANCIENT TIMES

The mediation process dates back to ancient times. It was used in both Phoenician and Babylonian commerce. The practice was further applied in ancient Greece, where a mediator was known as a *proxenetas*, and then in Rome starting from 530 to 533 CE, where a mediator was called *internuncius*, *medium*, *intercessor*, *philantropus*, *interpolator*, *conciliator*, *interlocutor*, *interpres*, and even *mediator*.

Certain defining characteristics from these sessions are still used in modern mediation, including

- the voluntary participation of both parties,
- the mediator being a neutral third party,

- the confidentiality of the mediation process, and
- a final, fair decision being reached by the disputing parties.

TIMELINE FOR ADR IN THE UNITED STATES

1920
▶ Enactment of the New York State arbitration statute, the first modern arbitration statute in the United States

1922
▶ The Arbitration Society of America is founded

1925
▶ Enactment of the United States Arbitration Act (Federal Arbitration Act)

1926
▶ The AAA is founded
▶ The AAA's National Panel of Arbitrators is created with 480 arbitrators
▶ Formulation of the Draft State Arbitration Act, which serves as a model for modern arbitration law
▶ Actors' Equity Association's basic minimum contract is one of the first industry contracts to include an arbitration clause wherein controversies arising between actors and managers are referred to the AAA

MEDIATORS BEYOND BORDERS

Mediators Beyond Borders—Partnering for Peace and Reconciliation is a nonprofit, humanitarian organization. It was established to work with communities worldwide in order to help them build their ability to prevent conflict, resolve conflict, and heal from conflict, using conflict resolution tools such as mediation.

Mediators Beyond Borders works across geographical, political, economic, societal, and cultural boundaries. It works in conjunction with nongovernmental organizations, universities, political and activist groups, community organizations, professional societies, and environmental, commercial, and other entities worldwide to help them develop skills that will facilitate public dialogue, collaborative negotiation, and public policy consensus building. In short, the organization uses mediation and other conflict resolution processes to prevent violence and to promote peace.

The organization maintains a presence in many current international disputes to raise awareness and promote the use of mediation to resolve them. One example was at the 15th Conference of the Parties to the UN Framework for Climate Change in Copenhagen on December 7, 2009, where the organization spread awareness on how mediation can be used in climate change and environmental disputes. Another was in October 2009, where the organization's Middle East Initiative collaborated with Wahat al Salam-Neve Shalom (Oasis of Peace) to develop a mediation curriculum to address the Arab-Israeli conflict specifically.

1931
▶ Publication of the First Code of Arbitration Practice and Procedure of the American Arbitration Association

1932
▶ The Accident Claims Tribunal of the AAA is established

1934
▶ The Inter-American Commercial Arbitration Commission is established

1936
▶ Membership in AAA's National Panel of Arbitrators reaches 7,000

1937
▶ The Voluntary Labor Arbitration Tribunal of the AAA is established
▶ The American Institute of Architects adopts a new arbitration procedure for standard building contracts and provides for its administration by the AAA

The History of Alternative Dispute Resolution

1938
▶ The first course ever in arbitration law is offered by New York University Law School

1940
▶ AAA facilities for Motion Picture Arbitration System in 31 cities in the United States created by consent decree

1941
▶ The American Defense Fund is established and the use of arbitration clause in munitions contracts is promoted

1944
▶ The Bureau of Labor Statistics reports that 75% of collective bargaining agreements in leading industries in the country provide for arbitration as the terminal point in grievance machinery

1945
▶ The first course ever in industrial arbitration is offered by New York University's Graduate School of Business Administration

1946
▶ Membership in AAA's National Panel of Arbitrators reaches 10,821
▶ Publication of AAA's Code of Ethics for Arbitrators
▶ A course in arbitration law is offered by Yale Law School

1947
▶ The Federal Mediation and Conciliation Service (FCMS) is established
▶ The first case goes to the International Court of Justice: *Great Britain v. Albania*, for destruction of British destroyers in Corfu Channel in the previous year

1948
▶ Labor cases now constitute over 62% of all AAA administered cases

1952
- An agreement is signed between the AAA and the Japan Commercial Arbitration Association providing for the use of arbitration clauses in Japanese-American trade contracts and for two tribunals in New York and Tokyo, where disputes may be resolved

1955
- The National Conference of Commissioners on Uniform State Laws gives final approval to a draft of the Uniform Arbitration Statute

1956
- The United Nations Economic and Social Council approves plans for a meeting in April 1958 aimed at furthering the development of arbitration in private law disputes as a measure beneficial to international trade; on the agenda will be a Draft Convention on the Recognition and Enforcement of Foreign Arbitral Awards
- The total AAA caseload numbers 2,817

1957
- Minnesota becomes the first state in the union to adopt the Uniform Arbitration Act
- Maine and Florida become the second and third states, respectively, to adopt modern arbitration laws

1958
- The United Nations Conference on International Commercial Arbitration takes place in New York; the central issue before the conference is the adoption of procedures for enforcement of international trade arbitration awards regardless of the place of arbitration or the nationality of the parties and arbitrators

1960
- In a series of three landmark decisions known as the Steelworkers Trilogy, the Supreme Court rules that doubts about arbitrability of labor–management grievances be resolved in favor of arbitration and that courts permit arbitrators to exercise flexibility in awarding remedies for violations of collective bargaining agreements

The History of Alternative Dispute Resolution

1966
- The total AAA caseload numbers 12,957

1968
- The AAA establishes its Center for Dispute Settlement to ease urban crises through arbitration, mediation, and fact finding

1970
- The United States ratifies the United Nations Convention on the Recognition and Enforcement of Foreign Arbitral Awards of 1958

1971
- Chief Justice Warren E. Berger speaks out in support of arbitration and the AAA in the July 1 issue of *Forbes*

1974
- The Supreme Court upholds international trade arbitration in its *Scherk v. Alberto-Culver* decision

1976
- The United Nations Commission on International Trade Law adopts the UNCITRAL Arbitration Rules for worldwide use
- The total AAA caseload numbers 35,156
- Membership in AAA's National Panel of Arbitrators reaches 37,000

1979
- The first National Women's Arbitrator Development Program, cosponsored by the AAA, the FMCS, and the New York State School of Industrial and Labor Relations, is established as a method of recruiting and training qualified women arbitrators

1981
- Inaugural ceremony for the United States–Iranian Claims Tribunal is held on July 1

1982
- Chief Justice Warren E. Berger issues a nationwide call for greater use of private arbitration as an alternative to litigation

▶ President Ronald Reagan signs a bill authorizing the arbitration of patent disputes

1984
▶ In *Southland Corp. v. Keating*, the Supreme Court rules that the United States Arbitration Act creates federal substantive law that is applicable in both federal and state courts and that supersedes conflicting state law in transactions evidencing commerce

1985
▶ In a landmark ruling (*Mitsubishi Motors Corp. v. Soler Chrysler-Plymouth, Inc.*) the Supreme Court holds that where a transnational contract contains a broad arbitration agreement, antitrust claims are arbitrable
▶ The UNCITRAL Model Law on International Commercial Arbitration is adopted at UNCITRAL's 18th session held in Vienna

1986
▶ The arbitrability of claims by investors against securities brokers is upheld by the Supreme Court in a major ruling handed down in *Shearson/American Express v. McMahon*
▶ Membership in AAA's National Panel of Arbitrators and Mediators reaches 60,000
▶ Total AAA caseload numbers 46,683

1990
▶ Enactment of the Administrative Dispute Resolution Act
▶ Enactment of the Civil Justice Reform Act
▶ Florida becomes the first state to require brokers to give customers the option of taking cases to the AAA rather than using an industry-sponsored forum

1991
▶ Putting forward the views of the Bush administration at the 113th annual convention of the American Bar Association, Vice President Dan

Quayle makes five specific recommendations for implementing ADR procedures; the suggestions emerge from a study by the President's Council on Competitiveness, whose Federal Civil Justice Reform Working Group made a total of 50 recommendations.

1993

- ADR comes into its own within the American Bar Association (ABA) with the creation of the ABA's Section of Dispute Resolution to replace its Standing Committee on Dispute Resolution

1994

- Martindale-Hubbell publishers introduce the new Martindale-Hubbell Dispute Resolution Directory, which lists approximately 70,000 arbitrators, mediators, judges, attorneys, law firms, and other neutral professionals who specialize in ADR
- The ABA Section of Dispute Resolution notes that most ABA-accredited law schools now offer ADR courses
- Total AAA caseload numbers 59,424

1995

- At a hearing of the Committee on Long-Range Planning of the Judicial Conference of the United States, AAA President William K. Slate II testifies that as the courts become inundated, the federal courts must be encouraged to consider and pursue alternative dispute resolution
- Membership in AAA's National Panel of Arbitrators and Mediators is culled to just over 27,350

AMERICAN ARBITRATION ASSOCIATION

The American Arbitration Association® (AAA) provides administrative services, both in the United States and abroad, to individuals and organizations who wish to resolve conflicts out of court.

The organization's services include assisting in the appointment of mediators and arbitrators, setting hearing dates, and providing its clients with information on the different dispute resolution options, including settlement through mediation. The organization's ultimate goal is to resolve cases through arbitration or mediation.

Additionally, the organization helps design and develop ADR systems to be used by corporations, unions, government agencies, law firms, and the courts. It also provides education, training, and publications to allow for a better understanding of the ADR process.

In 2009, the AAA created the A. Leon Higginbotham Jr. Fellows Program to provide training, mentorship, and networking opportunities to new and aspiring alternative dispute resolution professionals.

The AAA Higginbotham Fellows Program is a one-year program that offers the full scope of AAA resources to individuals who are interested in pursuing a future career in alternative dispute resolution. The program enables these individuals to participate and immerse themselves in all aspects of ADR (www.adr.org).

THE INSIDE TRACK

HON. ELIZABETH BONINA (RETIRED)
JUSTICE OF THE SUPREME COURT, KINGS
NATIONAL ARBITRATION AND MEDIATION (NAM)

When I retired as a judge, I wanted to continue using my legal expertise so I went into mediations and arbitrations. I have four professions—I am a part time judge, I have a small legal practice, I teach and I work at NAM. Of these four professions, mediation is what I like best. Why? Well, in mediation every case is different. There are different personalities involved, different difficulties to overcome. It's really fun! I also really appreciate the cost saving factor to the client. Although it can happen that you take some of the work with you home, it's just human, I think, to think about the cases when you come home, but I'm really good about not letting it bring me down.

Some of the cases that I have enjoyed the most are the ones where there was an extreme risk to both sides. Where the case could really go in either party's favor and where the result might be extremely detrimental to one of the parties. It's very satisfactory to be able to resolve those cases.

I would say there are two main techniques that work for me. I try to isolate the common ground. There are always some things that the parties can agree on. So let's isolate those factors and see what else we can find that we might be able to agree on.

The History of Alternative Dispute Resolution

The second technique I use is listening. It's such an important part of the process—to *really* listen.

I think having a legal background as a judge or lawyer is beneficial to the process. Part of our legal training is to remain impartial or professionally neutral. I think that's a necessary ability to bring with you in mediation.

The Theory of Alternative Dispute Resolution

CHAPTER three

IS LEGAL MEDIATION FOR YOU?

In this chapter, you will discover reasons to pursue a career as a legal mediator. What does the job entail? What does it offer? What are some of the skills you should posses in order to be successful as a mediator?

Out beyond ideas of wrong doing and right doing, there is a field.
I'll meet you there.
—Rumi

THERE ARE many reasons for entering the field of legal mediation. Mediators fulfill a vital role in the world of conflict resolution. They provide an opportunity to change the way societies handle conflicts.

Imagine a world where litigation was an absolute last resort and instead you relied on a mediator who knew you, understood you, your concerns, background, and issues, and aided you in resolving your dispute in a manner that kept all of these factors in mind. The more often disputes are resolved in mediation, the less likely people are to seek recourse in the court system, which inevitably pits people against one another in anger. Relying on mediation would change the entire system of conflict resolution as you know it. It would move us away from the litigious nature often resorted to and closer to a more amicable, compromising world.

The mediation field is very new and it takes a great deal of hard work, dedication, creativity, and perseverance to succeed in it. It also requires a sincere love of people and a genuine interest in listening with an objective mind in order to reach an amicable resolution. Depending on your area of specialization (see Chapter 4), you may also need to possess a thorough knowledge of a particular field.

There are many reasons you might enjoy a career in legal mediation. As noted in Chapter 1, mediators can work in a variety of environments: in private practice, within mediation groups, or in the court system, to name a few. Mediators have significant earning potential and some have the ability to be selective with the disputes they take on.

However, only approximately three quarters of those who complete mediation training end up practicing mediation. Some find the field to be unsuitable for them or discover they would not make good mediators after all. So, before you invest time and money entering the field, let us take a look at the motivation for would-be mediators and the personality traits of successful mediators.

MOTIVATIONS TO MEDIATE

Changing the World

Mediators use their skills to be of significant service in the world. Their work is deeply respected and has an effect that is widely felt. When disputing parties walk away from a conflict feeling heard and understood, it is a fufilling feeling for the mediator who helped them get to that point.

You have probably heard the term *litigious society*. When wronged by bosses, friends, coworkers, former partners, and so on, suing is a fairly common resort. Many people call lawyers to discuss the matter before they call the people they are in disagreement with. This is becoming an unfortunate trend.

In a courtroom, the people who are pitted against another party are by definition adversaries. In contrast, mediation parties are encouraged to sit down and discuss—rationally and reasonably—what may be a fair solution. In a courtroom, one party will win at the expense of the other party's loss. In mediation, people must find the compromise in the dispute. In a courtroom, a judge or a jury makes the decisions without any personal interaction with any party. In mediation, the disputing parties are inevitably personally responsible for the outcome of their mediation.

Mediation is not appropriate for every dispute; it is not a one-size-fits-all approach. But the fact is that it can save people money on lawyers and court costs; it can save time by resolving disputes faster than litigation, allowing disputing parties to get on with their lives; and it can certainly save people unnecessary anxiety. In mediation, people can resolve their disputes without losing those important human relationships that are often lost in the courtroom.

As a mediator, you will be helping to transform society in a profound way, by promoting concession and the human relationship over the concept of *being right*. The language of litigation has seeped into our social structure. Being a part of the mediation process means altering that language, updating its vocabulary to include words like *compromise* and *fairness*.

MEDIATION CASE: EXHIBIT A

In this example, pay attention to how the mediation process allowed each disputant to understand the other's position and to compromise in order to reach a final agreement.

The Seattle Federal Executive Board's ADR Consortium published an article called "Listening to Conflict (Mediation Case Study)" (www.mediate.com, September 2002) in which Mary, an administrative assistant at a government agency, was written up by her superior, Bob. The write-up occurred when Mary and Bob had a disagreement over an unfinished assignment. The disagreement turned into a heated argument that resulted in Mary's storming out of the office and going home for the day. Bob wrote Mary up for leaving the office without permission. Mary was concerned that if her employment file showed that she had been written up, she might be in danger of losing her job. Mary asked to have her case mediated in the hopes of having the letter rescinded.

In mediation, Mary was able first to convey how important her job was to her, especially as she was the sole breadwinner in her family. She was also able to explain that although she disapproved of Bob's management techniques, she took pride in her ability to support him. She was also able to convey that she felt Bob used inappropriate language and conducted himself unprofessionally when he was angry.

Bob was able to discuss his frustrations with Mary. He felt that she could be moody and erratic at times and sometimes questioned his authority. He also expressed that he appreciated and admired Mary's work ethic but had issued the letter because of her attitude. Finally, Bob, who is trained as a technician, talked about his frustration with his role as supervisor and the stress that the position has brought, especially when it came to dealing with employees.

After listening to each other and to the issues they each had, both Mary and Bob were able to make some useful changes. Bob told Mary that he would remove the letter after six months, if she improved her attitude. When Mary asked whether she could be granted time to take a class in conflict resolution to help her deal with work stress in a more effective manner, Bob even granted her tuition!

The open dialogue and frank communication enabled both parties to turn a bad situation into a positive one. The process allowed them to feel empowered to voice their concerns and find a solution they were both happy with.

Helping People

People who bring a dispute before a mediator do this because they truly want an end to the conflict, which might be painful, uncomfortable, or otherwise taxing. The mediator is able to help parties resolve their conflict.

A mediator does not tell people what to do. As a mediator, you have no ability to control what people decide. You do not make a decision for disputing parties and you cannot enforce your own values. However, an insightful question or remark is often all it takes to get disputants on the path toward a fair and fitting solution. And most mediators *agree* that this is the most satisfying part of the job. In the next example, a mediator helps a child come to terms with her parents' separation. Note how the child leaves the mediation feeling that she has been listened to by a neutral party.

MEDIATION CASE: EXHIBIT B

In a case study published by Family Mediation North Wiltshire, 9-year-old Nicole sees a mediator after her parents split up. Nicole had been demonstrating some behavior that had made her mother worrisome: she was suddenly very clingy and wanted to sleep in her mother's bed. At the mediation, it became clear that the separation had caused Nicole to experience a great deal of change: she had been forced to move, leaving her school and friends behind, and now was in a situation where her mother was home less in order to meet the demands of her new work schedule.

In mediation, a safe space was created for Nicole to express how she was feeling. She said that when her parents separated she felt as though "her heart had been split in two and that her dad had one half and mom had the other." She also told the mediator that she was aware of her mother's difficult financial situation and knew that her mother was anxious about bills coming when she went through her mail. Finally, Nicole told the mediator that she was very angry at her dad for leaving her mother for another woman and for causing her mother's financial concerns. But, at the same time, she missed her father and wished she could see him more often. Nicole was feeling torn between being angry with him and wanting to see him more.

The mediator told Nicole that she was not the only child who worries about her mother, but that taking care of the parent is not the child's job. Nicole seemed relieved to know that she was not the only one feeling this way and she now had permission to worry about herself. The mediator also helped Nicole see that having contradictory feelings toward her father was perfectly valid and that, in fact, such feelings can exist at the same time.

At the end of the mediation, Nicole stated that it felt good to talk about her problems, especially to someone who was not on either her mother's or her father's side.

LEGAL MEDIATOR SUITABILITY TEST

You say you want to be a legal mediator, but does the job suit you? To help you determine your answer, ask yourself these questions:

1. Do you enjoy listening to people's problems?
2. Do your friends and family members come to you often with their problems?
3. Do you handle pressure well?
4. Do you find that you keep your cool in stressful situations?
5. Do you have the ability to read people?
6. Do you express yourself well?
7. Are you patient?
8. Are you able to keep information confidential?

9. Can you make yourself understood by many different personality types?
10. Can you stay objective in a situation where you may become emotionally involved?

If you answered yes to most of these questions, then mediation is probably a very good choice for you. If you answered no to several of the questions, think about what draws you to to this field. You really have to be a *people person* and a good listener to be a successful legal mediator.

PERSONALITY TRAITS OF THE SUCCESSFUL MEDIATOR

There are several factors that will affect your ability to be a successful mediator and several personality traits that you should possess to be suitable for the job. Mediators come from many different walks of life; they have various skills, educations, and life experiences. However, a competent mediator is always an effective conflict manager. And competence depends on whether the mediator has the right mix of skills, training, and natural abilities to help resolve a specific dispute.

A mediation is successful when the two opposing parties find a way to cooperate. Mediators can facilitate cooperation even when they do not favor one or the other disputant but are able to keep an open mind as they assist the separate parties in their attempt to resolve the dispute. If the mediator or the opposing parties have an all-or-nothing approach, the mediation will most likely fail.

The most important skills and abilities for a mediator to possess are the ability to remain impartial, the ability to listen and communicate, and the ability to define and clarify issues.

Listening Skills

The ability to assess and help resolve the conflict depends on your ability to listen actively to the parties involved. Often you need to be listening to more than just the words; you need to be listening between the lines for the information that is being given indirectly.

How do you know whether you are a good listener? Pay attention to how you interact with others in a regular conversation. When you are listening to the other person talk, are you busy building an argument against what they are saying? Are you agreeing and waiting for them to stop talking so you can voice your agreement? Do you think you know what they are going to say next? Are you busy thinking about your next comment? Most regular conversations between people occur in this fashion.

Active listening requires that you create an open and inviting space for the speakers to voice their thoughts and concerns. Active listening requires your attention, eye contact, and open and friendly body language so that the speaker believes that your intention is truly to understand what is being said. This skill is a vital part of being a successful mediator.

Objectivity

As a mediator, your job is to suspend your own judgments and ideas. You are required to listen objectively to both parties and not allow your own personal beliefs or emotions to obstruct your listening.

Reaching an Understanding

As a legal mediator, you are trying to understand the two disputing parties, what their ultimate needs and wants are, and how best to get them to understand one another in order to reach an amicable resolution.

JAMS

Judicial Arbitration and Mediation Services (JAMS) is the largest private ADR provider in the world. It was founded in 1979 and employs more than 250 full-time neutrals such as mediators. Most of the cases that are heard at JAMS are complicated, multiparty cases within many legal specializations. JAMS handles about 10,000 cases per year and has offices all over the world. JAMS International, a subsidiary of JAMS, provides mediation and arbitration services to address cross-border disputes as well as international ADR training.

In 2002, JAMS created the JAMS Foundation and the JAMS Society. The JAMS Foundation provides grants for conflict resolution initiatives that have both national and international impact. The JAMS Society was created to support volunteer activities and community involvement for JAMS employees and associates (www.jamsadr.com).

ADDITIONAL QUALITIES OF THE LEGAL MEDIATOR

In his 2008 article "Doing the Best Mediation You Can," John Lande, associate professor and director of the LLM (Master of Laws) Program in Dispute Resolution at the University of Missouri Law School, discusses some findings uncovered by the Task Force on Improving Mediation Quality (Task Force) of the ABA section of Dispute Resolution, which collected information from focus groups of actual disputants.

The Task Force concluded that disputing parties were most impacted by the following four factors:

1. the preparation stage between the mediator and the disputants,
2. the mediator's ability to customize the mediation process,
3. careful consideration of any analytical assistance that the mediator may provide, and
4. the mediator's persistence and patience.

Preparation before Mediation Sessions

Most of the study's participants said that the mediation really begins during the preparation phase. During this stage, the parties *should have an appropriate understanding of the process, the issues, and their real interests.*

The preparation stage should be used by the mediator as a time to identify the parties' goals. Although most participants said that settling the case and minimizing the time, cost, and risk are important goals, many added that satisfying the parties' underlying interests is also an important goal in most cases. Many disputants use this stage to tell their stories, feel heard, reach closure, promote communication between parties, and preserve relationships.

Case-by-Case Customization of the Mediation Process

Study participants generally said they wanted a mediation process that was tailored to their needs rather than a standardized formulaic procedure. Many participants noted that they appreciated getting coaching from mediators about the process. The customization process would allow for the special needs of each of the parties to be accommodated. For example, it is typical for each party to give an opening statement; however, if the parties' relationship is particularly hostile or disagreeable, insisting on an opening statement may be counterproductive. Mediators who try a one-size-fits-all approach may end up losing some of the confidence needed to help resolve the matter at hand.

Careful Consideration about Providing Analytical Assistance

Almost all of the mediators and participants said that mediators can be helpful by asking pointed questions and suggesting options to consider, but some participants expressed concern over mediators who use more controversial techniques, such as making predictions or recommendations or applying pressure.

MEDIATION TECHNIQUES

Mediators use a variety of different techniques in order to enable the disputants to reach a resolution. Some mediators have an understanding of these tools through the training they have had. Others are just intuitive coaches.

Visioning is a technique that allows the mediators to help the parities see what objectives they share, where they have a common goal. Once it is established that the parties actually can agree on some things, the mediator can then help the parties discover what else they might be able to agree on.

Problem solving is a technique the mediator may use to help the disputants define their problem and then try to come up with problem-solving techniques that may work.

Neutral language is a technique that allows the mediator to ask the parties to use language that will promote, as oppose to hinder, creativity and forward movement in the dispute. When the disputants start to use negative, emotional language to communicate fears and anger, the opposing party will get defensive and communication will be blocked. Neutral language allows the mediator to diffuse highly emotional issues into productive negotiations.

Acknowledging is a coaching technique that uses language that makes the disputants feel they have been heard and understood.

Attending is a technique that uses body language to communicate to the disputants that they are being paid attention to.

Affirming is a coaching technique whereby the mediator gives the disputants positive feedback, for example, *that's a great point, tell me more about that.* Affirming lets the parties know that what they have said has value.

Probing is a coaching technique that mediators employ to obtain additional information from the parties. The mediator might ask probing questions to uncover what is really at the heart of the disputants' conflict.

Reflecting is a communication skill a mediator will use to assure the parties that he or she is clear on what is important to them. In reflecting, the mediator paraphrases the disputants' statements and repeats it to them.

Reviewing is a coaching technique by which the mediator goes over the main points of a discussion. The mediator reviews what has just happened in the session between the two parties and determines whether the parties are ready to move forward. Reviewing can happen at any point in the mediation, but it is especially useful when the mediation has already taken several days.

Persistence and Patience

An overwhelming majority of participants said that a mediator's ability to be patient and persistent was extremely important. Participants were dissatisfied when mediators gave up too easily. It is when the opposing parties are most antagonistic that the mediator should work the hardest to help people overcome their challenges. If a mediation session ended without agreement but had some potential to reach one, most participants felt that the mediator should have offered additional help.

THE SUCCESSFUL LEGAL MEDIATOR'S TOOLBOX

- **Overall people skills**

You must have an earnest belief in the basic goodness of people and the ability to communicate with others effectively. You must be able to earn your clients' trust by proving yourself to be someone who is attentive, impartial, and able to suspend judgement.

- **Good verbal and listening skills**

You must have the ability to listen actively, giving your full attention to the matter at hand and listening for the truth between the lines. You need to be able to hear what people are saying as well as what they are leaving out.

- **Creative thinking**

Much of your success as a legal mediator will lie in your ability to come up with creative solutions that may fall outside of the norm. Coming up with creative solutions will require that you spend time reflecting on your case and the disputants involved. Jessica L. Stock, Esq. of NAM explains that she has seen cases resolve when a mediator makes an unlikely suggestion. For example, in one medical malpractice case, the mediator suggested that a memorial monument be erected or a scholarship fund be started in memory of the deceased.

- **Impartiality**

The ability to be impartial is an absolute must for the legal mediator. In your work, you may find yourself being more sympathetic to one party than to another. It is vital that you remain impartial, objective, and fair in all of your endeavors as a mediator.

- **Respect for the parties**

Being respectful of the parties in the dispute is an important element in an effective process. You must be able to respect both parties' dignity and competence regardless of the nature of the dispute. You can show this in the simplest of ways: polite behavior, engaging body language, handshakes, and patience. Most importantly, you can show your respect for the parties by making them all feel you are not judging them but accepting them.

- **Knowledge of the mediation process**

The mediation process is not a highly ritualized, multistep process that requires strict adherence to the rules and regulations of the procedure. Instead, you will need to prove your knowledge of the process by demonstrating your abilities as an attentive listener, a creative problem solver, and a quick study of the facts of the dispute.

- **Initiative and the confidence to use it**

The mediator is inevitably in charge of the outcome of the mediation. You must be confident in your knowledge of the rules of the procedure as well as in your ability to help bring the parties to an amicable resolution.

- **Trustworthiness**

During the mediation process, there will be times when the opposing parties share confidential, personal, and sometimes embarrassing information with you. It behooves you to keep such information to yourself. If you are unable to do so, you will quickly find that you establish yourself as an untrustworthy mediator.

- **Ability to remain calm under pressure**

Sometimes mediations can turn ugly. Sometimes the opposing parties are just too angry to reach any conclusion that would make the mediation successful. In such cases, you must remain calm, and consider the possibility that mediation is an inappropriate forum for this dispute.

CAREER DRAWBACKS

The field of legal mediation is not one that garners much prestige. Mediators work hard and the job may not seem glamorous. A mediator's time is spent actively listening to people complain about various issues, some of which may be trying to the mediator. Each workday can seem grueling, filled with many complaints, issues, and disputes—not an easy job at all!

Many mediators start out excited to be of service and to help people with their conflicts, only to find the work extremely difficult after a few years. The most obvious difficulty is that it can be very taxing and emotionally draining to listen to people's problems for hours at a time. It is very common to see mediators who express excitement at the beginning of their careers quickly become mentally exhausted from the pressure. To the mediator who is a good fit for this job, this intense responsibility is offset by the joy of having been of a tremendous help to people in their time of need.

Isolation

Mediators often work alone. Even those who work within mediation groups typically handle each mediation alone. There are no coworkers to complain to, no social interaction with peers, and no one in the desk next to you to whom you can voice your concerns and frustrations. If a particular case is especially difficult, it is yours to handle alone.

Helper Role

A mediator's job is to help people reach conclusions on their own. A mediator's hands are tied if he or she cannot get the parties to reach a viable conclusion.

Limited Positive Feedback

It is rare that the parties in mediation will thank their mediator for his or his work. Most often, they are very much absorbed in their own dispute, their own hurt, and their own anger. Even when the mediation ends in an agreement, the parties involved have each made some concession, so there may be some residual bad feelings, which would prevent them from having the emotional clarity to be gracious to the facilitator of the mediation.

Confidentiality

A mediator is often privy to very private information regarding the parties involved. It is vital to the integrity of the process that the mediator keep this information private. This can be a hard task for some mediators who might feel they need to discuss the case with others in order to help mediate.

Filtered Reaction Role

Do you remember the last time you were having a conversation with someone and you reacted negatively to something that was said? Maybe you became angry, frustrated, or hostile. These are all reactions that may well come up in a mediation. You may be annoyed at something one of the parties says, you may disagree with them, or find them irresponsible. As a mediator, it is your job to avoid responding to these emotions and instead deal with the parties involved in an impartial manner.

WHAT IF MEDIATION DOES NOT WORK?

There will be times when no matter what you try, you cannot get the parties to settle. Often this happens when there is just too much hostility and anger between the parties to agree on anything. Other times, one party may have suffered so much—whether perceived or actual—that no amount of logic, reasoning, or technique will allow them to move on.

For those instances in which mediation does not lead to an agreement or resolution, you want to make sure you have done everything you can as the mediator. Did you talk to the parties in private? Did you explain the disadvantages of going to court? Did you follow up with them after they left to see whether they had a change of heart once they had had a chance to digest all the information?

If you have tried all you could and the case is still not settling, you need to make sure that the parties know what their rights are going forward. They have the right to try to address their dispute in some other manner; perhaps they might have more luck in arbitration. The parties can also choose to litigate their case, that is, take it to court. If the parties do go to court, the mediator cannot be called to testify nor can the records or notes of mediation be entered into evidence.

Finally, if you have done everything you can, it is time to let the case go. Do not hold on to it as a failure. There is a new set of disputants who need you to have the strength and peace of mind to try it again.

The Mediator's Professional Liability

Similar to lawyers, doctors, and other professionals, a mediator's conduct is held to high standards. Therefore, mediators need to understand where

Is Legal Mediation for You?

they are most vulnerable in terms of liability issues and protect themselves accordingly. This can prove to be a difficult task, since there is currently no clear mediator job description, nor an established standard that can be used to compare against the received service. The easiest liability issues to identify include giving inaccurate information or failing to give sound advice regarding the best way to resolve a dispute. If a mediator recommends mediation in a case that is clearly inappropriate for that process, the mediator may be held liable. Another liability problem revolves around the issue of a breach of confidentiality. Confidentiality in mediation is not just a matter of ethics, it can lead to serious consequences, including court proceedings.

The three areas where a mediator may have liability issues are as follows.

1. **Liability in Contract**
   Liability in Contract happens when the mediator breaches the contract between him/herself and one or more of the disputants. There are two ways the mediator can breach a contract; one is called a failure to perform and the other is an anticipatory breach. If it can be proven that the mediator has actually breached the contract (which is much harder to do in the latter example as the breach has not happened yet), the mediator may have to pay damages.

2. **Liability in Tort**
   Liability in Tort happenes when a mediator influences one of the disputants in an improper way, such as making derogatory remarks about the other party or sharing confidential information to push a decision. In order to be compensated, the wronged party must show that the mediator's actions had a negative result for the disputant.

3. **Liability for Breach of Fiduciary Obligations**
   Liability for Breach of Fiduciary Obligations happens when the mediator behaves in a way that causes the parties to believe that the mediator's role is not that of a neutral third party; for example, if they believe the mediator to be their legal advisor.

The best ways to protect yourself as a mediator is to make sure you are completely comfortable with the process and that you have had a good amount of training and experience. Also, as mediation is becoming a more mainstream profession, liability insurance products have started to become available to help absorb some of the risks that come with the work.

THE INSIDE TRACK

HON. JOHN P. DIBLASI (RETIRED)
JUSTICE OF THE SUPREME COURT, WESTCHESTER
NATIONAL ARBITRATION AND MEDIATION (NAM)

As a trial attorney I saw three important factors. First, the incredible uncertainty clients have to deal with when leaving a decision up to a jury. No one can predict what a jury is going to do. You would have better luck going to Atlantic City and trying to predict the outcome at the slot machines than trying to predict what a jury will do. Second, is the incredible amount of time it takes for cases to go though the courts and the amount of time the client has to wait for resolution. Third, the immense costs to the client in court fees and legal expenses. Then as a justice of the Supreme Court I saw a repeat of all three factors. In my time as a judge I saw some judges who actively managed their calendars, who would try to get the case resolved before going to trial, and others who saw it as their sole responsibility to try cases.

After being a trial attorney and justice of the Supreme Court for fifteen years, I can say that I am enjoying myself now more than ever. In my work now I am actually solving problems, not creating them. Mediation is an amazing field. I love it!

CHAPTER four

SPECIALIZATION WITHIN THE LEGAL MEDIATION FIELD

Most mediators recommend that you find a niche for yourself within the field—a special area of demand for a product or service—that both interests you and that there is a need for.

It is astonishing how elements which seem insoluble become soluble when someone listens. How confusions which seem irremediable turn into relatively clear flowing streams when one is heard.
—Carl Rogers

MEDIATORS ARE often in high demand when the economy is slow, because people and businesses try to save money on lawyers and lawsuits by looking for other low-cost ways to resolve conflicts. On the other hand, there can often be an overabundance of mediators, because the requirements to gain access into the field are low. This is where thinking ahead can be in your best interest. What are your skills, and how can you apply them to the current or, better yet, future economic situation?

Finding a niche does not mean that you will be tied to a particular specialty for life, nor does it mean that you will have to turn down mediations in areas outside of your specialty. In fact, over time, you may expand your niche to include new areas of expertise.

The mediation field is wide and the profession is extremely versatile, so your specialty choice is completely up to you. However, there are some very important benefits to having a niche. Perhaps the most important of these benefits is that having a niche will allow you to target your marketing to a specific audience. (See Chapter 8 for more information on marketing). You will be able to narrow down your publicity and advertising to be most productive. If your marketing is directed at too wide a field, you will come across as a kind of general contractor of mediation rather than as an expert in your field. People trust the expert; they want a specialist to mediate for them. Another benefit of being a niche mediator is that you will be recognizably different from other mediators. This will allow you over time to establish a reputation in the field. In general, establishing a niche allows you to focus your energy, time, and resources on mediation success.

FINDING YOUR NICHE

One of the advantages to entering the mediation field is that this industry allows you to bring your past experiences with you. These experiences might include your education, your life skills, and your previous work know-how.

To find the niche that suits you the best, inventory the skills and knowledge you already have and find the mediation area that those skills align with. By doing so, you will use the contacts, knowledge base, skill set, expertise, and reputation you have already acquired. For example, if your experience has been in the medical field, you might want to specialize in healthcare negotiations or in medical mediation between boards of directors in hospitals and healthcare professionals. If you have been a stay-at-home parent for a while, perhaps a specialization in family matters would suit you. Is your background in financial services, education, or social work? All these specialties can be transformed into niches within your legal mediation career.

If you have selected a mediation specialty, take a moment to ask yourself the following questions, which will help you decide whether this niche is really for you.

1. Are you passionate about this niche?
2. Do you already know, or are you interested in learning, something about this niche?

Specialization within the Legal Mediation Field

3. Are there actual problems that need resolving within your proposed niche?
4. Is there a market for your niche in the area where you plan on practicing?
5. Are there many other mediators in your area already specializing in your niche?
6. Do you have a unique trait, attribute, or skill that would help you succeed in this niche?
7. Does your specialty already have other people working within it; that is, are there industry magazines, unions, groups, forums, and the like available?

FAMILY MEDIATION

Mediation is a widely used practice in the family court system. Mediators are often assigned by the courts in order to protect a child's best interest. Commonly, a mediator handles matrimonial matters such as divorces. In a divorce situation, a mediator can help keep the discussion focused on the matters at hand—alimony, terms of the separation agreement, custody, visitation—and not spend time rehashing issues that led to the divorce. The family matters mediator navigates through an emotional and difficult time with the disputing parties, so they can identify the solutions that best meet their individual needs as well as the needs of the entire family.

SUBCATEGORIES WITHIN FAMILY MATTERS

Mediation in family matters includes

- premarital agreements,
- prenuptial, financial, or budget disagreements,
- separation,
- divorce,
- financial distribution and spousal support (alimony),
- parenting plans (child custody and visitation),
- eldercare issues,
- family businesses,
- adult sibling conflicts,
- disputes between parents and adult children,
- estate disputes, and
- medical ethics and end-of-life issues.

Divorce Mediation

Because divorces so often take place before a mediator, the mediator usually meets the opposing parties early on in the process. This can be both helpful and harmful. It can be easier when the parties are new to the process. They are not yet frustrated and have not yet spent large sums of money on failed agreements. On the other side, it is often the most difficult time for the disputing parties. The decision to separate might be new, and fears or doubts may start to surface. For these reasons, it is important that the mediator be particularly well trained. Many states that offer mediation as part of the family court system have stringent mediator qualification requirements.

Due to the sensitive nature of a divorce mediation both parties may decide to retain individual attorneys to support them at the mediation by consulting with them about legal rights and advising them on their specific situation. This approach can lead to peaceful, personal, and private solutions that most often save time, money, and stress.

When a divorce meditation takes place later in the process, it is usually because money and time have been spent without reaching any kind of conclusion. At this point, the already fragile relationships are worn thin and usually a great deal of anger has arisen. Such mediations are often much more challenging to bring to a viable conclusion.

Divorce mediations may take place with several parties present. The mediator typically meets with the two disputants alone at first, but the attorneys for each party may also choose to be present. Sometimes other professionals such as child development professionals, real estate professionals, and financial professionals may be present depending on the intricacies and complexities of each case. Typically, the attorneys are present to protect their parties' financial interests, while the mediator focuses on such matters as parenting, custody, and visitation.

The Difference between Divorce Mediation and Litigation

	Mediation	Litigation
Average rate	$2,000–$5,000	$20,000 per person
Average time involved	3 to 6 months	2 years

Specialization within the Legal Mediation Field

The Difference between Divorce Mediation and Litigation *(continued)*

	Mediation	Litigation
Impact on children	children's interests are central to decision-making	children are often caught in a battle between the parents
Confidentiality	sessions and financial forms are confidential	court hearings and financial forms are public

Mediators have varying styles and are free to conduct the mediation in the way they see most fit. Some factors, however, must be present in order to maintain the integrity of the process.

The Common Thread in Divorce Mediation
- ▶ The mediator must maintain impartiality at all times. The mediator's voice is to be neutral between the husband and the wife.
- ▶ The mediator may not give legal advice to either party.
- ▶ The mediator must remind both spouses openly what they are trying to accomplish so that the spouses are free to negotiate with each other rather than dwelling on the issues that led to the divorce.
- ▶ The mediation continues only as long as all the parties deem it effective, necessary, and desirable. The mediator may choose to end the mediation if there is a good reason why the case is not appropriate for mediation. The disputing parties may withdraw for no reason at all.
- ▶ The mediation will take less time, cost less money, and be less emotionally taxing than an adversarial divorce.
- ▶ The mediator's job is to keep the parties in control of their own divorce. This can have a major effect on the parties' ability to move on with their lives. In addition, the fact that the parties are in charge of the proceeding allows for a greater level of communication, more understanding, and less conflict.

Your Goals as a Divorce Mediator
- ▶ to protect the relationships within the family
- ▶ to allow the individuals involved in the conflict to leave the mediation with their self-respect intact and feeling in control of their lives

- ▶ to foster a positive relationship between the disputants so that they can effectively coparent
- ▶ to allow the parties to focus on the potential for the present and the future, not the past
- ▶ to maintain confidentiality, impartiality, and focus
- ▶ to facilitate an amicable resolution in this very difficult and emotional time

Child Custody Mediation

Mediation can be especially useful when the parents who are separating are unable to reach an agreement about the best arrangement for their children. Within the mediation process, the children's feelings and wishes are part of the final agreement. The aim is not only to make the best of the fractured relationship between the adults but also to salvage the relationship between the parents and the children.

Many studies have been conducted about children and their response to a divorce. Donald T. Saposnek, a clinical child psychologist, and author of the article "How Are the Children of Divorce Doing?" points out that it is not the actual separation that is most damaging to the child. Rather, it is the way the opposing parties handle themselves during the matter. A divorce process inherently heightens emotions and can make it very difficult to behave with consideration, especially when there is a child involved. Often the child is impacted negatively by the high levels of emotions and stress that cause parents to make poor decisions. In child custody mediation, the mediator will have a child consultation with the consent of both parents. The goal of a child consultation is to enable the parents to understand the wishes of the child. Because the child feels understood and heard, the amount of damage felt by the child is minimized.

Benefits of Child Custody Mediation

- ▶ The very nature of the mediation process is that it is nonadversarial. It focuses on maintaining the relationships at stake. A nonadversarial

Specialization within the Legal Mediation Field

process is less stressful and less emotional for all. When emotions and stress levels are kept in check, the process is significantly easier on the children.
- ▶ A child custody settlement is mutually and voluntarily agreed to in mediation. This typically means that the parents will be more likely to abide by the terms of the agreement. Also, because the parents must work together to create the agreement, groundwork is laid for future cooperation. In an adversarial court preceding, on the other hand, the judge decides the terms of the agreement, making it more likely for the losing party to fight it or default on it, and blocking the opportunity for communication between the disputants in the future.
- ▶ Mediations cost less money and takes less time than going to court.
- ▶ Child custody mediation is collaborative. Everyone has a voice and everyone is heard. The child's wishes are paid attention to, allowing the child to feel empowered and a part of the process as well as fostering cooperation between the parents. Mediation allows for a custody arrangement that considers the individual factors of each particular family. All parties can leave the mediation feeling empowered.

Clearly, there are many benefits to settling a dispute involving child custody in mediation. In certain instances, however, child custody mediation is inappropriate such as when the family has a history of conflict and there is a large degree of mistrust between the parties. Mediation will also be ineffective if one or both parties are fearful of the other, or when parties do not have an open exchange. Under those circumstances, the mediator may recommend that the case be resolved in a different forum.

Alimony

Determining who gets to keep what after a divorce is finalized is often considered the most challenging part of a divorce. Many people think that the collaborative nature of mediation may make this an ineffective way to handle an alimony dispute. In actuality, however, mediation affords a powerful opportunity for divorcing parties to reach an amicable solution. The open nature of the mediation process allows the participants to consider information and data that they both have access to, so they can come to a realistic conclusion based on actual and mutually shared information.

The overarching job of the mediator in alimony cases is to help the parties develop an economic plan that is reasonable for each party.

EMPLOYER–EMPLOYEE MEDIATION

Over the last 20 years, the courts have championed the ideas of equal opportunity and fair employment in employer–employee disputes. However, lawsuits arising from such disputes are expensive, time-consuming, and disruptive. This has led to the need for alternative ways to resolve these conflicts, making employer–employee mediation another excellent choice for new mediators.

Many companies encourage and even insist on mediation before they resort to litigation. One main reason for this is that disputes between businesses and employees can be severely damaging to all parties involved. A major public dispute with a key executive of a company can harm that company's reputation. When an employee makes a claim against his or her current or former employer, mediation is valuable because of its confidential nature. In mediation, the details of the dispute will not be made public, saving the reputation and name of the company and also lessening the potential embarrassment for the employee. In mediation, both parties have the opportunity to communicate their real interests, which vastly increases the potential for resolving the conflict.

THE MOST COMMON EMPLOYER–EMPLOYEE CONFLICTS

Employer–employee conflicts frequently arise when
- an existing employee feeling harassed by a supervisor, or
- a terminated employee or an existing employee who is denied a promotion feels that the decision was made for inappropriate reasons, such as race, color, religious affiliation, national origin, age, or disability.

Specialization within the Legal Mediation Field

Many business and companies include some formal method of conflict resolution within the infrastructure of the organization—internal complaint, investigation, peer review, nonbinding mediation, and finally, arbitration. These steps are often written into employment contracts, manuals, and employee handbooks. There are several reasons for this. Employees are happiest and most productive if there is some fair, reasonable, and efficient method for hearing their grievances. Most people spend the greatest portion of the day in the workplace. When an internal method for conflict resolution exists, employees' job satisfaction and productivity are greatly affected.

Another reason for having an internal mediation system in place is that the U.S. Supreme Court has passed recent decisions requiring that employers maintain some kind of reasonable and fair method for hearing employee grievances.

BENEFITS OF IN-HOUSE EMPLOYER–EMPLOYEE MEDIATION PROGRAMS

The U.S. Supreme Court has decided upon a number of ways in which employers can protect themselves when faced with sexual harassment and other discrimination claims from employees. First, the employer can demonstrate that reasonable measures have been taken to prevent the harassment or discriminatory behavior. Another way is by showing that the employee did not take advantage of programs made available by the employer to resolve these matters.

In instances where it is claimed that workers were harassed by their supervisors, for example, the employee does not need to prove that the employer was negligent, nor does the employee need to have reported the harassment. By offering in-house mediation services, an employer can show that company programs are in place to address the conflicts arising out of such conduct.

Because of the private and informal nature of the process, the safe environment the process provides, and the repair to relationships that result, many businesses will seek out mediators both on staff and as outside contractors. And as a mediator in this niche, you will have the potential for a steady stream of interesting cases to mediate.

LANDLORD–TENANT MEDIATION

Although lease agreements are drawn up and agreed to before the landlord–tenant relationship begins, it is not uncommon for disputes to arise when the parties fail to fulfill their general obligations or when the parties have a different understanding of the language in the agreement. Both tenants and landlords have general obligations in the relationship. The tenant's responsibilities include making sure they pay rent on time, avoiding damaging the landlord's property, and not subleasing without permission. In return, the landlord needs to ensure that ordinary wear and tear repairs are made; the living space is habitable; water, gas, and electricity are available; and the tenants are not discriminated against. When these general obligations are not met, a dispute may occur.

Landlord–tenant disputes are a great mediation niche for a few reasons. First, the disputants are interested in keeping costs low and having the case resolved quickly, making them more likely to look to mediation. Second, since such disputes happen frequently, a mediator specializing in these matters is most likely to have a large volume of cases to mediate.

Steps in Landlord–Tenant Mediation

Introduction
The landlord and the tenant come to the mediation and tell their side of the story. The mediator instructs them that they need openly to listen to the views of the other disputant, come up with their own ideas for reaching an amicable conclusion, and be willing to negotiate a settlement agreement.

Agenda Building
The mediator helps the disputants list the issues that they need to have resolved in order to reach a settlement. Each party lists the issues that are of most concern to them.

Negotiation
The mediator discusses the interests of each party and starts to develop and suggest options that address these interests. The mediator starts to think of

ways to create a workable, mutually satisfactory agreement—one that attempts to maintain the relationship between the disputants.

Meetings
Depending on the level of hostility between the parties, the mediator may decide to conduct private meeting with the individual disputants. The information shared in these private meetings—known as caucuses—will not be shared with the other party without consent.

Agreement
Once the mediator has helped the disputants reach an agreement, it is put in writing and signed. The terms of the agreement must be written in the disputants' own words and be considered reasonable by both parties. If no agreement can be reached the mediator may suggest other forms of conflict resolution.

PERSONAL INJURY MEDIATION

When someone is injured as a result of someone else's negligence or carelessness, the injured party has a personal injury claim. Often, but not always, a personal injury claim is brought against an insurance company.

Personal injury mediation is a type of formalized negotiation between the injured party and the negligent party. The mediator oversees the negotiations between the disputants and facilitates the arrival at a resolution. In a personal injury matter, the mediator's aim is to help the disputants come to an agreement, which usually involves an amount of compensation that is considered fair. Such cases can be difficult, because it is difficult to decide what amount of money is fair for an injury to an eye, for example, or for long-term back pain. The injured party living with the pain may feel that a large sum of money is fair, while the insurance carrier may make arguments that diminish the extent of the physical damage. The goal for the mediator is to allow the disputants to come to a mutually agreeable compromise, where the insurance company or the negligent party agrees to compensate the injured parties, and the injured party agrees to accept this compensation.

When the parties agree to mediation, they agree to participate in the process with the mediator and with each other. Because mediation is voluntary, the parties may decide to stop the mediation at any time if they feel they cannot resolve their dispute in this manner. If the disputants do come to an agreement and sign it, they are legally bound by it.

What makes personal injury mediation a good niche? Personal injury mediators, have access to a large number of new cases. One reason for the high volume is that personal injury mediation is promoted by the court. Mediation is usually requested, and sometimes required, by a court before a case can be scheduled for trial to enable the disputants to resolve their dispute in this manner first.

Another reason is that injured parties understand that it is far more beneficial for them to choose to mediate because they often need their settlement money quickly and with the smallest expenditure. The injured party may have medical bills to pay, or may remain unable to work, and needs the settlement money for living expenses.

CONTRACT MEDIATION

Agreements between business partners or between businesses and customers are fleshed out in a contract in advance of the actual transaction in order to ensure that both parties are clear as to what their responsibilities are and what they can expect from the other party. However, it is not uncommon for one party to feel wronged because they disagree on the interpretation of the language in the contract or because they feel the other party has violated the contract.

Why would mediating business contracts make a great niche? Mediating contracts has become a commonplace occurrence. In fact, most contracts require that, should a dispute arise, it must be heard via some form of ADR process before litigation can take place. Businesses are seeing the many benefits that come from resolving disputes in mediation; this circumstance is leading to an increased demand for mediators who specialize in contract matters.

The most obvious benefit is the cost factor. Mediation costs are usually shared and are minor in comparison to litigation.

Another benefit is that neither party has to lose. The goal in mediation is to have both parties leave feeling they have come to a win-win solution. The end result is that the business relationship need not be destroyed as a result of the dispute.

Finally, the disputants are more likely to adhere to an agreement drafted in mediation because they were able to collaborate in drafting it. Although the mediation is voluntary and there is no obligation for either party to stick with the process until the matter has been resolved, an agreement, once made, is binding.

Mediation used in a business setting has shown some impressive results. Kenneth P. Kelsey, the director of commercial operations for Daimler-Benz Transportation, states that *over 80% of the disputes that are voluntarily submitted to mediation are satisfactorily resolved. And, even for court-referred mediations, over 50% are settled satisfactorily without burdening the court system.*

Deciding Fairness

Mediation is an excellent way to resolve just about any contractual dispute, especially one where there is no legal question per se, but more a feeling that one party has not been fair. For example, parties in a construction case presenting a *delay claim*—meaning that they feel they should be compensated for the extended length of time it took the contractor to finish a job—are appealing for an adjustment to their contractual terms because of fairness, not for negligence or any other legal rule.

If mediation cannot reach a conclusion, the parties may still choose to litigate the case. Even then, the mediation process has not been wasted, because some parts of the dispute may have been narrowed down and resolved, leaving the larger, irreconcilable issues up to a judge or jury.

MORTGAGE MEDIATION

Because of the current weak economy, the failing housing market and the problems associated with subprime mortgage lending, many homeowners are unable to meet their mortgage obligations. In this climate, mortgage renegotiation may be a specialty worth considering. Mortgage renegotiation mediation entails stepping in between the homeowner, who might be in danger of defaulting, and the bank.

As a mediator, you would help renegotiate the terms of the mortgage agreement, allowing the homeowner a chance to avoid foreclosure. During nationwide mortgage crises, mediators are in high demand as they relieve some of the pressure from the ever-increasing docket load. The courts often encourage disputing parties to rely on mediators to resolve their disputes.

In his article, "Court Urged to Require Foreclosure Mediation," Mark Killian discussed a petition that was presented to the Supreme Court by private attorneys, which requested that mediation be made available in all foreclosure cases. He states that prejudgment mediation could save more than 130,000 Florida homes from foreclosure and assist more than 360,000 Florida borrowers.

ADR AT WORK IN GOVERNMENT

Congress passed the Administrative Dispute Resolution Act of 1996 to acknowledge that resolving disputes had become costly, ineffective, and time consuming, and to authorize the implementation of ADR tools within federal agencies. Noting that the private sector had been successfully using various forms of ADR, the Act sought to encourage the use of ADR within the public sphere to help resolve disputes arising between government agencies, such as the United States Department of Justice and the individuals and organizations with which they do business.

The federal government then established the Alternative Dispute Resolution Working Group to facilitate the use of ADR tools and processes in government agencies. The group has been divided into several subcategories to address the many different needs of government agencies.

One subcategory is the Workplace Conflict Management section, which addresses employer–employee relations within government agencies. The Workplace section helps different government agencies use conflict management processes to prevent, address, and resolve all types of employment-related conflicts in the federal workplace.

Another subcategory is the Claims against the Government section, which attempts to resolve claims against a federal agency where the opposing party is seeking monetary damages. Any federal agency may set up an ADR program to resolve disputes before a lawsuit is started.

Specialization within the Legal Mediation Field

CREATING YOUR NICHE

Over time, the mediation process has proven to be an effective way to handle many different types of disputes. Each different case type represents an opportunity for the mediator to specialize or to create a niche. Mediators who specialize in a specific area have even been used in courts to hear cases that fall within their area of expertise, leaving the courts free to deal with issues that require the full due process of law.

As a mediator, you can create your own niche. If you see the need for a specialization that does not yet exist, by all means go for it. However, if you would prefer the security of specializing in already established areas, some are more appropriate for mediation than others. These areas include family matters, employee–employer, landlord–tenant, personal injury, contract issues, and many other non-criminal matters.

Most mediators will tell you that the secret to a successful mediation practice is to specialize, specialize, specialize. Choose a niche that fully utilizes your skill set and that you already know something about. Most importantly, choose a niche that you enjoy and that you see yourself continuing to enjoy far into your career.

THE INSIDE TRACK

JESSICA LEE STOCKTON, ESQ.
VICE PRESIDENT OF COMMUNICATIONS AND DEVELOPMENT
NATIONAL ARBITRATION AND MEDIATION (NAM)

When I was doing my undergraduate work at Boston University, I really struggled with the decision for my major. I always had law school in the back of my mind but I was also interested in art history and I didn't think an art history major would be useful for my legal aspirations. But at orientation I met a professor, who later became my art history professor, who told me that there was such a thing as art law and that I could absolutely apply what I learned in my undergraduate studies to my career as a lawyer. After graduating from Boston University, I went to Quinnipiac University School of Law. After graduating from there, I practiced law for a very short amount of time before I became interested in mediation. I heard about a master's degree program at Pepperdine University and called them to hear about how to apply. They told me that the application deadline was actually that day! They agreed to grant me a week long extension to get all my paperwork in and I got accepted. Looking back at it now, I realize that it was the best decision I ever made. I am completely in love with the mediation process—it's just so cool! I absolutely love my work. Once I graduated I went to work for Lucile Barron who really mentored me and taught me everything I know about the business. She was not a lawyer; she was a woman who went through a messy divorce where she felt she had been overcharged by her attorneys. She went through the mediation process to recoup some of her money and was so excited about the process that she started her own mediation company. Then I got this opportunity with NAM where I get to run the business side of things and I love it! The mediators will sometimes come out of the mediation and express frustration that they are not getting the case to settle and I say, "Just keep them here, keep them talking." I love being a part of the process.

CHAPTER five

CREDENTIALING AND TRAINING

To date, there are no federally imposed rules regarding the education necessary to become a mediator. This can be both a positive and a negative thing. The bad news is that since the field is so accessible, you may be faced with a great deal of competition. The good news is that you can set yourself ahead of the competition fairly easily, with credentialing or training.

Don't find fault. Find a remedy.
—Henry Ford

AT PRESENT, there are no formal, federally mandated educational requirements for prospective mediators. Various states have different rules about the qualifications needed, and many private mediation organizations require that you have some training before they allow you to sit on their panel. Often, private mediation groups impose their own curriculum and training program that you must complete before you can mediate a case for them. For example, the AAA requires mediators to complete a training course that includes an apprenticeship and also requires recommendations from the trainers.

Even though there is no formal rule, there are a few reasons to consider training, licensing, or credentialing when you enter the legal mediation field. First, as a mediator you are charged with a serious and important task.

Most mediators would argue that you will be best equipped to handle the job if you have had some kind of training before you do you first real mediation. Second, because the field is fairly accessible, many people try to become mediators. Having some training or credentialing will set you apart from many others when you are job hunting.

PUBLIC MEDIATING JOBS

If you are interested in applying for a mediation job within the court system or in some city, state, or federal agency, you will find that most states will require you to have some training, certain certifications, or extensive time on the job. There are many benefits that come with holding a public position. In the court system, you will have a steady stream of cases to mediate without having to worry about doing your own marketing. Also, you will work significantly fewer hours as a public employee than if you work for a private institution. In addition, public jobs have a great deal of job perks, such as a pension, extensive medical benefits, and job security.

If you are interested in a public mediation job, the list following state-by-state will explain what requirements you need to meet depending on the state where you will be looking for employment. Remember, the qualifications listed are applicable only to mediators seeking court employment. Courts will often allow the disputing parties to choose their own mediators who are not on the court-approved lists, but you must meet these requirements if you are looking to be an employee of the court system.

Alabama

There are no state requirements for the practice of mediation. The Alabama Center for Dispute Resolution maintains the State Court Mediator Roster for public information about mediators who meet their qualifications.

Qualifications for the general roster include

- good character,
- being a licensed attorncy (any state) with 4 years of practicing law, or having served professionally as the mediator in 10 cases in the preceding 2 years,

- ▶ 20 hours of approved mediation training,
- ▶ subscribing to the Code of Ethics and rules, and
- ▶ providing 10 hours annual pro bono upon request.

Qualifications to be registered as a domestics relations mediator include

- ▶ good character,
- ▶ one of the following previous professional experiences:
  - ▶ being a licensed attorney (any state) with 4 years of practicing law,
  - ▶ being a licensed physician in good standing by the state, certified in the practice of adult or child psychiatry,
  - ▶ being a certified public accountant (CPA) licensed by the state and in good standing, with 4 years of practicing accountancy,
  - ▶ being engaged in a practice for 4 years in social work, mental health, or behavioral sciences, with a bachelor's or advanced degree in one or more of these fields,
  - ▶ having served professionally as the mediator in at least ten mediations, at least five of which are domestic relations disputes, within the 2 years immediately preceding submission of an application for registration,
- ▶ taking an approved 40-hour mediation course on domestic relations,
- ▶ subscribing to the Code of Ethics and rules, and
- ▶ providing 10 hours annual pro bono upon request.

Alaska

There are no state requirements for the practice of mediation.

Arizona

There are no state requirements for the practice of mediation. Each county court has its own set of requirements for mediators. All require at least 40 hours of basic mediation training, plus additional training in family law for those who mediate family cases.

Arkansas

There are no state requirements for the practice of mediation.

The Arkansas ADR Commission has established the following categories of guidelines dealing with mediator skills and qualifications:

- general guidelines for the public to use in selecting a mediator,
- standards and procedures for being placed on the voluntary roster of mediators maintained by the Commission, and
- standards that may be used by the courts in establishing court-annexed mediation systems or selecting court-referred mediators (courts are not required to follow the ADR Commission's guidelines or to use mediators from the roster).

Requirements for inclusion on the voluntary roster of mediators include

- having a bachelor's degree,
- 40 hours of approved mediation training,
- having observed, comediated, or mediated two mediation sessions,
- good moral character, and
- accepting and following the Guidelines for Conduct of Mediation and Mediators.

Guideline qualifications for family mediators include

- 40 hours of approved family mediation training or 40 hours of general mediation training plus 20 hours of family or parenting mediation,
- having a bachelor's degree and 2 years' experience in family and marriage issues; a master's degree in social work, mental health, or behavioral social science; or being an attorney,
- having observed, comediated, or mediated two family mediations,
- good moral character, and
- accepting and following the Guidelines for Conduct of Mediation and Mediators.

Guideline qualifications for small-claims courts include

- 16 hours of approved small-claims court training,
- good moral character, and
- accepting and following the Guidelines for Conduct of Mediation and Mediators.

Guideline qualifications for circuit or chancery courts for other than family matters include

- 40 hours of approved training,
- being a member in good standing of the Arkansas bar or having a master's degree,
- having observed, comediated, or mediated two mediation sessions in circuit or chancery courts,
- good moral character, and
- accepting and following the Guidelines for Conduct of Mediation and Mediators.

California

There are no state requirements or guidelines, except for child custody mediation through the courts. Qualifications for child custody mediators in court cases include

- having a master's degree in counseling, social work, or a related field, or having experience above the minimum in these fields,
- 2 years of experience in the mental health arena or education or training above master's degree, and
- 16 hours of continuing education annually.

Individual courts may establish additional requirements.

Colorado

There are no state requirements for the practice of mediation.

There are guidelines endorsed by the Colorado Bar Association (CBA) and the Colorado Council of Mediators and Mediator Organizations on mediator training and education. Additionally, there are voluntary Colorado Standards of Conduct for Mediators endorsed by the Office of Dispute Resolution (ODR), the Colorado Judicial Institute, the CBA, the ADR Forum Committee, and the Attorney General's Office, Department of Law. The Office of Dispute Resolution does not maintain a roster. However, the ODR does contract with mediators in each district to provide services.

The following are recommended qualifications for mediators who contract with the Office of Dispute Resolution:

- 40 hours of mediation training,
- having mediated 20 cases, preferably solo cases in courts in a substantive area of practice,
- substantive knowledge of law,
- familiarity with the court system,
- a nondirective mediation style,
- meeting the needs of the program,
- being acceptable to the court and to local attorneys,
- being willing to assist with local development of ADR programs,
- fitting in with the local team, and
- residing near local program and having minimal scheduling conflicts.

In addition, mediators who are offered a contract with the ODR may be required—at their own expense—to complete an internship, including an observation and critique by a group of their peers, known as a peer review observation, and comediation.

Connecticut

There are no state requirements for the practice of mediation. Each civil clerk's office and court information desk maintains a public listing of private

ADR providers but does not make referrals. Court-annexed mediation primarily uses retired judges as mediators. Mediation training is not required; however, the Superior Court publishes a list of Superior Court senior judges and judge trial referees, who have attended mediation training sessions.

Delaware

There are no state requirements for the practice of mediation. The Delaware Superior Court maintains a roster of neutrals for court referrals. The roster requires *new attorneys or other qualified professionals* to take 25 hours of training in conflict resolution techniques approved by the president judge of the Superior Court. Mediators are asked to complete five pro bono mediations to complete their training and to assist the court. Disputants are encouraged to participate in the court's mediation program.

District of Columbia

There are no state requirements or guidelines for mediation in a private setting. Mediators in the courts must be staff or volunteers of the Superior Court Multi-Door Dispute Resolution Division's Mediation Program.

Qualifications for small-claims mediators include

- successfully undergoing a selection orientation to assess each candidate's communication style,
- 40 hours of approved training,
- comediating with several mentors until approved as a probationary mediator,
- performing an agreed number of hours of mediation through the program, and
- undergoing performance evaluations.

Qualifications for family mediators include

- successfully undergoing a selection orientation to assess each candidate's communication style,

- 55 hours of approved training,
- comediating with several mentors until approved as a probationary mediator,
- performing an agreed number of hours of mediation through the program, and
- undergoing performance evaluations.

Qualifications for civil court mediators include

- being a licensed attorney,
- being an active or inactive member of the bar of any U.S. jurisdiction,
- completing 27 hours of approved training,
- completing 6 hours of pro bono mediation,
- mediating approximately 17 cases during a 12-month period, and
- participating as required by the program in performance assessment and in-service training.

Florida

There are no state requirements for the practice of mediation. Parties may choose any mediator, subject to the approval of the judge. The State Supreme Court maintains a list of certified mediators. Mediators must be on the list to receive court referrals. All certified mediators must be of good moral character.

Qualifications for county court mediators include

- observing four county court mediation conferences conducted by a certified mediator,
- conducting four conferences supervised by certified mediator, and
- completing 20 hours of certified mediation training.

Qualifications for family mediation mediators include

- having a master's in social work, mental health, or behavioral or social sciences; being a physician certified in psychiatry; being a licensed at-

torney or a CPA from any U.S. jurisdiction with 4 years of experience in the field; or having 8 years of family mediation experience with a minimum of 10 mediations per year,
▶ observing two family mediations conducted by a certified family mediator,
▶ conducting two family mediations supervised by a certified family mediator, and
▶ 40 hours of certified training.

Qualifications for circuit court mediators for other than family matters include

▶ being a member in good standing of the Florida bar with 5 years of Florida practice and being an active member of the Florida bar within 1 year of application, or being a retired trial judge from any U. S. jurisdiction having been a member of the state bar for the preceding 5 years,
▶ observing two circuit mediations conducted by a circuit-certified mediator,
▶ conducting two circuit court mediations supervised and observed by a certified circuit court mediator, and
▶ 40 hours of certified training.

Qualifications for dependency mediators include

▶ having a master's in social work, mental health, or behavioral or social sciences; being a physician licensed for psychiatry or pediatrics; or being a licensed attorney from any U.S. jurisdiction,
▶ observing four dependency mediations conducted by a certified dependency mediator,
▶ conducting two dependency mediations supervised by a certified mediator, and
▶ 20 hours of certified training under the supervision of a certified family mediator who has mediated four dependency cases; otherwise 40 hours.

Georgia

There are no state requirements for the practice of mediation when a court case has not been filed. However, all neutrals working on court cases must be registered with the Georgia ODR. The ODR maintains a list of registered mediators but does not make referrals. Courts are free to impose higher qualifications for neutrals who serve in their programs than the threshold requirements for registration with the ODR.

Overall guidelines state that mediators should be drawn from a variety of disciplines and should reflect the racial, ethnic, and cultural diversity of our society. Prospective mediators should also be screened carefully for qualities such as the ability to listen actively, to isolate issues, and to focus discussion on issues.

General mediator qualifications for ODR registration include

- observing or comediating with a veteran mediator in at least five mediations,
- one letter of recommendation from a court ADR program, other approved ADR provider, or a superior or state court judge; or three letters of recommendation from clients, attorneys of clients, court personnel, or registered neutrals who have observed the applicant's performance as a neutral, and
- 20 hours of training.

Qualifications for divorce and custody case referrals include

- satisfying the requirements for general mediators,
- having a bachelor's degree from an accredited 4-year college,
- observing one mediation and comediating two divorce/custody cases with a veteran mediator, and
- 40 hours of domestic relations training, including training on domestic violence.

Hawaii

There are no state requirements for the practice of mediation. The Center for Alternative Dispute Resolution has published voluntary Standards for

Private and Public Mediators in the State of Hawaii, endorsed by the Supreme Court. The standards call for mediators to have substantive knowledge and procedural training, including professional ethics, standards, and responsibilities. Mediators must also acquire continuing education.

Idaho

There are no state requirements for the practice of mediation. The Supreme Court Administration Director of Courts maintains two rosters of mediators: a Civil Case Mediator Roster and a Child Custody Mediator Roster.

Qualifications for the Civil Case Mediator Roster include

- ▶ being a member of the Idaho State Bar, and
- ▶ having been admitted to practice law for no less than 5 years and attended a minimum of 40 hours of approved training.

Additionally, mediators are required to complete 20 hours of approved continuing education every 2 years to remain on the roster.

Qualifications for the Child Custody Mediator Roster are any one of the following professional credentials:

- ▶ membership in the AFM at the practitioner level, or other national organizations with equivalent standards for membership,
- ▶ being a member of the Idaho Judiciary, a licensed member of the Idaho State Bar Association, a licensed psychologist, a licensed counselor, a certified social worker, a certified school counselor, or a certified school psychologist who has attended a minimum of 40 hours of mediation training, 20 of which were in the field of child custody mediation, or
- ▶ having a bachelor's degree with a minimum of 60 hours of mediation training, 20 of which must be in the field of child custody mediation.

In addition, mediators must complete 20 hours of continuing education every 2 years.

In Idaho, a private or public dispute resolution organization may make its roster of mediators available to the Administrative Director of the Courts for distribution if it has an established selection and evaluation process, a mechanism for addressing complaints brought against neutrals, and a published code of ethics.

The Idaho Mediation Association (IMA) has made its list of Certified Professional Mediators available; the list is distributed by the Administrative Director of the Courts. IMA requirements for certification include

- current and continuing membership in the IMA,
- 40 hours of core mediator skills and knowledge training,
- 20 hours of mediation case practice,
- 60 hours of additional mediation-related experience or study,
- a letter of recommendation for professional certification by an IMA-certified professional mediator or the professional equivalent, and
- 20 hours of continuing education every 2 years.

Illinois

There are no state requirements for the practice of mediation. The use of ADR in the Illinois court system is decided on a circuit-by-circuit basis. The qualifications for mediators vary among circuits.

Indiana

There are no state requirements for the practice of mediation. Disputing parties may choose any mediator with the approval of the court. The Indiana Supreme Court Commission for Continuing Legal Education maintains the Registry of Qualified Mediators for court practice.

Qualifications for mediator registration in civil cases include

- being an attorney in good standing with the Indiana Supreme Court,
- 40 hours of approved training,

- ▶ 6 hours of continuing education every 2 years, and
- ▶ conforming to ethical requirements established by ADR Rule 7.

Qualifications for registration in domestic cases include

- ▶ having a bachelor's degree from an accredited university,
- ▶ 40 hours of approved training,
- ▶ 6 hours of continuing education every 2 years, and
- ▶ conforming to the ethical requirements established by ADR Rule 7.

Iowa

There are no state requirements for the practice of mediation. Two of the eight judicial districts in the state have ADR programs. To qualify as a family mediator, the mediator must meet the ethical standards set by the AFM and receive 40 hours of divorce mediation training.

Kansas

There are no state requirements for the practice of mediation. The Kansas Judicial Branch Dispute Resolution Coordinator maintains a list of approved mediators for court referrals and referrals by state government.

General qualifications for listing include

- ▶ 16 hours of core mediation training plus additional hours for the types of cases the applicant wishes to receive approval to mediate,
- ▶ signing an agreement to follow the ethical standards of Supreme Court Rule 903,
- ▶ comediating with or being supervised by an approved mediator for three cases or 15 hours during the first year following core training, and
- ▶ 6 hours of continuing education annually.

Qualifications to mediate domestic disputes include

- ▶ satisfying general qualifications,
- ▶ 14 hours of mediation skill training, and
- ▶ 10 hours of subject matter training.

Qualifications to mediate parent–adolescent disputes include

- ▶ satisfying general qualifications,
- ▶ 14 hours of mediation skill training, and
- ▶ 10 hours of subject matter training.

Qualifications to mediate general civil cases of a nondomestic nature include

- ▶ satisfying general qualifications,
- ▶ 14 hours of mediation skill training, and
- ▶ 10 hours of training related to the subject being mediated or the civil litigation system.

Kentucky

There are no state requirements for the practice of mediation. Administrative Office of the Courts are beginning to develop standards that they hope will be adopted by the Supreme Court or the state legislature in the near future.

Louisiana

There are no state requirements for the practice of mediation.

The ADR Section of the Louisiana Bar Association maintains a register of persons qualified as mediators pursuant to La. R.S. 9:4106 (civil cases) and La. R.S. 9:334 (child custody and visitation). Disputing parties, attorneys, and judges are encouraged to select a mediator from the register, but are not required to do so.

Credentialing and Training

Qualifications for inclusion on the register for civil cases include

- ▶ being licensed for the practice of law in any state for 5 years and having completed 40 hours of approved training; having mediated more than 25 disputes or engaged in more than 500 hours of dispute resolution and completing 40 hours of approved training *or* having served as a Louisiana district, appellate, or supreme court judge for 10 years, but no longer serving as a judge,
- ▶ 10 hours of continuing education every 2 years, and
- ▶ accepting 2 pro bono appointments annually.

To serve as a qualified mediator in child custody and visitation cases, a candidate must either

- ▶ have served as a Louisiana district, appellate, or supreme court judge for at least 10 years, have completed at least 20 hours of specialized mediation training in child custody disputes, and no longer be serving as a judge, or
- ▶ possess a college degree and complete a minimum of 40 hours of general mediation training and 20 hours of specialized training in the mediation of child custody disputes, or
- ▶ hold a license or certification as an attorney, psychiatrist, psychologist, social worker, marriage and family counselor, professional counselor, or clergyman and complete a minimum of 16 hours of general mediation training and 20 hours of specialized training in the mediation of child custody disputes.

In some cases, mediators must also complete a minimum of 8 hours of comediation training under the direct supervision of a qualified mediator who has served a minimum of 50 hours as a dispute mediator. Mediators must also complete a minimum of 20 hours of clinical education in dispute mediation every 2 calendar years.

To serve as a qualified mediator in a juvenile court dispute pursuant to Louisiana Children's Code article 439, a candidate must either

- ▶ possess a college degree and complete a minimum of 40 hours of general mediation training and 20 hours of specialized training in the mediation of juvenile court disputes, or

- hold a license or certification as an attorney, psychiatrist, psychologist, social worker, marriage and family counselor, professional counselor, or clergyman and complete a minimum of 16 hours of general mediation training and 20 hours of specialized training in the mediation of juvenile court disputes.

In some cases, mediators must also complete a minimum of 8 hours of comediation training under a course that has been approved by the Louisiana State Bar Association, Alternative Dispute Resolution Section, or under the direct supervision of a mediator who has served as a dispute mediator for a minimum of 50 hours. A minimum of 20 hours of clinical education in dispute mediation must also be completed every 2 years.

Maine

There are no state requirements for the practice of mediation.

The Court Alternative Dispute Resolution Service (CADRES) of the Maine Judicial Branch maintains mediation rosters. Court referrals must be made from the appropriate roster. The CADRES director may waive qualification criteria for a particular applicant.

Qualifications for General Civil Litigation Roster include

- having a combination of 100 hours of training and experience, including a minimum of 40 hours of mediation process training (15 hours within 2 years of application), 20 hours of experience as mediator or comediator with a CADRES mediator, and 10 hours of training in civil law and court procedure, and
- 15 hours of continuing education annually in specified areas.

Qualifications for Superior Court Roster include either

- being on the CADRES General Civil Litigation Roster, or
- having a combination of 100 hours of training and experience, including a minimum of 40 hours of mediation process training (15 hours within 2 years of application), 20 hours of experience as media-

tor or comediator with a CADRES mediator, and 10 hours of training in civil law and court procedure.

Mediators must also have the ability to conduct mediation, receive a satisfactory criminal background check, complete a half-day orientation and training program on the Superior Court ADR Program, and finish 15 hours of annual continuing education in specified areas.

Qualifications for the Small-Claims Roster include either

- ▶ a combination of 50 hours of training and experience, including a minimum of 20 hours of mediation process training (8 hours within 2 years of application) and 15 hours of experience as a mediator of multiparty contested issues,
- ▶ comediation with a CADRES mediator and 3 hours of training or experience in consumer or debtor–creditor law.

Mediators must also complete 8 hours of continuing education annually in specified areas.

To qualify for the Environmental, Land Use, and Natural Gas Pipeline roster, candidates must have a combination of 110 hours of training and experience. The 110 hours include a minimum of 40 hours of mediation process training (15 hours completed within 2 years of application), 15 hours of experience as a mediator or comediator with a CADRES mediator, and 20 hours of work experience or substantive training in a land use or environmental field. Candidates must also complete CADRES land use mediation training and 15 hours of continuing education per year in specified areas.

Maryland

There are no state requirements for the practice of mediation.

Each county administrative judge prepares an approved list of mediators for court appointments. Generally, qualifications include

- ▶ being 21 years of age,
- ▶ having a bachelor's degree from an accredited university (this requirement may be waived for good cause),

- ▶ 40 hours of approved training,
- ▶ abiding by a code of ethics,
- ▶ agreeing to submit to periodic monitoring, and
- ▶ complying with the court's procedures, including accepting reduced-fee or pro bono cases.

In addition to meeting the qualifications above, mediators of child access disputes must also observe two custody or visitation mediations conducted by an approved mediator and complete 20 hours of approved training in family mediation.

Massachusetts

There are no state requirements for the practice of mediation.

The Chief Justice of each trial court department approves programs to receive court referrals. The Chief Justice for Administration and Management combines and distributes these lists.

Basic qualifications for mediators include

- ▶ 30 hours of basic mediation training,
- ▶ court orientation,
- ▶ specialized training if required for a trial court department,
- ▶ evaluation in a role-play situation,
- ▶ observing a minimum of one mediation under the supervision of a qualified mediator and discussing the mediation with the mentor,
- ▶ being observed mediating a minimum of one case and discussing the mediation with a mentor, and
- ▶ continuing education.

Michigan

There are no state requirements for the practice of mediation.

Each court creates its own list for court referrals. Many courts have developed referral processes with local community mediation centers. Generally, mediator qualifications include

- 40 hours of training,
- observation of or participation in two mediations, and
- 8 hours of continuing education every 2 years.

The qualifications for domestic relations mediators who provide services under this program include

- completing a training program approved by the State Court Administrator,
- observing two domestic relations mediation proceedings conducted by an approved mediator, and
- conducting one domestic relations mediation to conclusion under the supervision and observation of an approved mediator.

In addition, a domestic relations mediator must be a licensed attorney, a licensed or limited licensed psychologist, a licensed professional counselor, or a licensed marriage and family therapist; have a master's degree in counseling, social work, or marriage and family therapy; have a graduate degree in a behavioral science; or have 5 years of experience in family counseling.

Minnesota

There are no state requirements for the practice of mediation.

The Office of Supreme Court Continuing Education maintains two separate rosters: civil and family. In court-ordered mediation, the parties, attorneys, or judges must choose from these rosters. To qualify for the Civil Facilitative and Hybrid Neutral roster, a candidate must complete 30 hours of training, which includes 15 hours of role-playing, in specified areas.

Qualifications for the Family Law Facilitative Neutral roster include

- 40 hours of certified family mediation training in specified areas, with 40% dedicated to role-playing and simulations,
- 6 hours of domestic abuse mediation training, which may be part of the 40 hours above, and
- good standing in the mediator's profession.

Mississippi

There are no state requirements for the practice of mediation.

A list of mediators is maintained by the Mississippi bar. Courts and parties are encouraged—but not required—to select mediators from this list.

To qualify for this list, a candidate must be a member of the Mississippi bar in good standing and complete 14 to 16 hours of training approved by the court-annexed mediation committee.

Missouri

There are no state requirements for the practice of mediation.

Individual courts may maintain lists of mediators, utilize lists maintained by a bar association, and establish mediation programs.

To practice in a circuit court program for civil cases, a candidate must complete 16 hours of training.

To practice in a circuit court program for child custody and visitation cases, a candidate must be an attorney or have a graduate degree in psychiatry, psychology, social work, counseling, or another behavioral area substantially related to marriage and family interpersonal relationships. Candidates must also complete 20 hours of training.

Montana

There are no state requirements for the practice of mediation.

The clerk of the Supreme Court maintains three lists of resident Montana attorneys who have indicated their desire to be appointed as mediators in appeals cases. For court appointments in appeals cases, listed attorneys must be members in good standing with the State Bar of Montana and have been licensed as attorneys for no less than 5 years.

Nebraska

There are no state requirements for the practice of mediation.

The state recognizes six ADR centers, each with its own mediator qualifications. In order for a center to receive state funding, its mediators must complete a minimum of 30 hours of training. For disputes involving marital dissolution, mediators must have an additional 30 hours in family mediation. A three-session apprenticeship with an experienced mediator is required for all candidates without prior mediation experience.

Nevada

There are no state requirements for the practice of mediation. Each court may develop its own mediator qualifications.

To participate in the court-connected mandatory access and visitation mediation program of the Eighth Judicial District Court, a candidate must

- hold a law degree or a master's degree in psychology, social work, marriage and family therapy, counseling, or a related behavioral science,
- complete 60 hours of approved child custody and divorce mediation training, including a minimum of 4 hours of domestic violence mediation training,
- possess 3 years of experience in the domestic relations arena conducting child custody mediation,
- finish 15 hours of continuing education each calendar year, and
- adhere to the Model Standards of Conduct for Mediators.

New Hampshire

There are no state requirements for the practice of mediation.

The New Hampshire Marital Mediator Certification Board maintains a list of certified marital mediators.

Qualifications for certification are

- 60 hours of approved training, including 8 hours of domestic violence issues and 15 hours of direct role-play,
- a 60-hour internship, involving six different marital mediation cases with a certified marital mediator and 54 hours in comediation with a certified marital mediator, and
- three recommendation letters from people who have participated with the candidate in marital mediation work.

In addition, recertification is required every 3 years.

Court referrals are made from a directory. To be listed in the directory, a candidate must be an attorney approved by the court, with 20 hours of court-sponsored training in civil mediation, and adhere to the Guidelines for Rule 170 Mediators.

Qualifications for practicing in the probate courts are

- 5 years of experience as a mediator,
- 40 hours of training, and
- the ability to travel regionally.

Knowledge of the probate court is highly desired.

New Jersey

There are no state requirements for the practice of mediation.

Qualifications for civil, general equity, and probate mediators include

- an advanced or undergraduate degree in the field of intended mediation practice,
- 5 years of professional experience in the field of intended mediation practice,
- two mediations in the last year if the candidate has an advanced degree, or 10 mediations in the last 5 years if the candidate has an undergraduate degree,
- 18 hours of training in specified areas,
- 4 hours of continuing education annually, and
- good professional standing.

Qualifications for custody and parenting time mediators are

- a graduate degree or certification in a behavioral or social science,
- supervised clinical experience in mediation,
- 40 hours of training in specified areas,
- 4 hours of annual continuing education, and
- good professional standing.

Credentialing and Training

The assignment judge may substitute relevant experience for education, clinical experience, or both.

Special civil part mediators (small-claims and landlord–tenant) must complete 12 hours of approved training.

New Mexico

There are no state requirements for the practice of mediation.

Recommended qualifications for family courts are 40 hours of basic mediation training and 16 hours of training in abuse and neglect mediation.

Recommended qualifications for state agency mediators are 40 hours of basic mediation training, 20 hours of mentoring, and 20 hours of facilitation.

New York

There are no state requirements for the practice of mediation.

Qualifications for community mediators are

- 25 hours of training and role-play conducted by a certified trainer,
- completing one observation and two mediations under the supervision of the program director,
- 6 hours per year of continuing education, and
- conducting three mediations per year to remain active in the program.

Additional qualifications for family mediation are 12 hours of training in visitation and custody and/or adult–child area of specialty.

North Carolina

There are no state requirements for the practice of mediation.

Qualifications for certification for civil cases for attorneys include

- 40 hours of certified mediation training,
- being either a member in good standing of the North Carolina State Bar, or being a member in good standing of the bar of another state

Becoming a LEGAL MEDIATOR

and demonstrating familiarity with North Carolina courts and procedures and providing two reference letters,
- 5 years of legal experience,
- observing two mediated settlement conferences conducted by a certified mediator, one of which must be court ordered,
- demonstrating familiarity with the statute, rules, and practice governing mediated settlement conferences in North Carolina, and
- being of good moral character and adhering to ethical standards.

Qualifications for certification for civil cases for nonattorneys are

- 40 hours of certified mediation training,
- 6 hours of certified training on North Carolina courts and related matters,
- three reference letters,
- observing five mediated settlement conferences conducted by at least two different certified mediators (one of which must be court ordered) and demonstrating familiarity with the statute, rules, and practice governing mediated settlement conferences in North Carolina, and
- good moral character and adherence to ethical standards.

In addition, nonattorneys need one of the following:

- 20 hours of basic mediation training and mediating 30 disputes over 3 years or equivalent experience, and a 4-year college degree or 4 years of management or administrative experience, or
- 10 years of management or administrative experience.

Qualifications for certification for equitable and other family financial cases for attorneys include

- 40 hours of certified mediation training,
- either being a member in good standing of the North Carolina State Bar or being a member in good standing of the bar of another state and demonstrating familiarity with North Carolina courts and procedures and providing three letters of reference,

Credentialing and Training

- 4 years of legal experience,
- observing five mediated settlement conferences conducted by a certified mediator, three of which must involve custody or family financial issues,
- demonstrating familiarity with the statute, rules, and practice governing mediated settlement conferences,
- good moral character and adherence to standards of practice, and
- continuing education.

Qualifications for certification for equitable and other family financial cases for nonattorneys include

- being an advanced practitioner member of the Association for Conflict Resolution (ACR),
- 6 hours of certified training on North Carolina courts and related matters,
- three reference letters,
- observing five mediated settlement conferences conducted by a certified mediator, three of which must involve custody or family financial issues,
- demonstrated familiarity with the statute, rules, and practice governing mediated settlement conferences,
- good moral character and adherence to standards of practice, and
- continuing education.

North Dakota

There are no state requirements for the practice of mediation.

The state court administrator maintains rosters for civil mediation and domestic relations and contested child proceedings mediation.

Qualifications for the civil mediator roster include

- 30 hours of training with specified components,
- 15 hours of role-play, and
- 9 hours of continuing education every 3 years.

Qualifications for the domestic relations and contested child proceedings mediator roster are

- ▶ 40 hours of domestic relations training, including 2 hours on domestic abuse mediation,
- ▶ a bachelor's degree in behavioral science with 2 years of experience in family–child intervention service; a master's degree in behavioral science with 1 year of experience in family–child intervention service; or a license to practice law with 2 years of experience in domestic relations cases, and
- ▶ 9 hours of continuing education in domestic relations training every 3 years.

Ohio

There are no state requirements for the practice of mediation.

Local practice requires a minimum of 40 hours of mediation training for civil mediators in the courts of general practice.

Mediators who are employed by the court or to whom the court makes referrals in disputes concerning parental rights and responsibilities are required to meet the following qualifications:

- ▶ a bachelor's degree or equivalent educational experience,
- ▶ 2 years of professional experience with families,
- ▶ 12 hours of basic mediation training or equivalent experience as a mediator, and
- ▶ 40 hours of approved specialized family or divorce mediation training.

Oklahoma

There are no state requirements for the practice of mediation.

Certification is granted when a candidate has obtained

- ▶ approval by a certified program,
- ▶ 20 hours of training with specified components,

Credentialing and Training

- written recommendation from the trainer,
- observation of one mediation by a certified mediator,
- written approval of the sponsoring program's coordinator,
- 10 hours of annual service as a mediator or comediator in a certified program with satisfactory evaluations, or equivalent continuing education, and
- recertification each fiscal year.

Certification as a family and divorce mediator is granted when a candidate has obtained

- approval by a certified program,
- signed commitment to provide 8 hours of service per month or 80 hours of service per year as a mediator, training coach, mentor, peer evaluator, or other service,
- 40 hours of training with specified components,
- written recommendation from the trainer,
- mediation and/or comediation of three to five actual family and divorce mediations (minimum of 12 hours) supervised by a certified mediator,
- written approval of the sponsoring program's coordinator,
- 80 hours of annual service as a mediator or comediator in a certified program with satisfactory evaluations (continuing education may be substituted for some hours), and
- recertification each fiscal year.

Minimum qualifications for civil and commercial mediators are either to be certified pursuant to the Dispute Resolution Act or all of the following:

- observing two mediation proceedings,
- 24 hours of approved training,
- 6 hours of continuing education every 2 years, and
- adhering to the Model Standards of Conduct.

Minimum qualifications for divorce and family mediators are either to be certified pursuant to the Dispute Resolution Act or all of the following:

- having been regularly engaged in the practice of family and divorce mediation for 4 years,

- ▶ completing 40 hours of training in family and divorce mediation and conducting 12 hours of mediation with three separate families,
- ▶ 6 hours of continuing education every 2 years, and
- ▶ adhering to the Model Standards of Conduct.

Oregon

There are no state requirements for the practice of mediation.

Qualifications for community dispute resolution program mediators include

- ▶ 30 hours of training with three supervised role-plays,
- ▶ an evaluation, and
- ▶ Two supervised mediations.

Qualifications for family matters mediators include

- ▶ 30 hours of mediation training with three supervised role-plays and evaluation, plus 24 hours of domestic relations training,
- ▶ a master's degree with substantial coursework in behavioral science, or a law degree, with seminar or graduate-level work in specified family issues,
- ▶ 20 supervised domestic relations mediations, 2 years as a mediator, or 2 years of counseling or legal experience with six cases or 60 hours of mediation case experience, and
- ▶ 12 hours of continuing education per year.

Qualifications for mediators specializing in the financial aspects of family matters, such as alimony and child support, are the same as the above with the addition of

- ▶ 40 hours of family legal and financial training, including 6 hours of role-play and six supervised financial mediation cases, and
- ▶ 7 hours of continuing education per year.

Pennsylvania

There are no state requirements for the practice of mediation.

The Pennsylvania Supreme Court established minimum qualifications for mediation in custody and visitation cases through family court programs and court-ordered mediation for individual cases. Local courts may impose additional, more stringent qualifications.

Minimum qualifications include

- a bachelor's degree and practical experience in law, psychiatry, psychology, counseling, family therapy or any comparable behavioral or social science field,
- the successful completion of approved basic training in domestic and family violence or child abuse mediation and a divorce and custody mediation program,
- mediation professional liability insurance,
- additional mediation training, consisting of a minimum of four mediated cases totaling 10 hours under the supervision of a mediator who is approved by the court to supervise other mediators,
- compliance with the ethical standards of the mediator profession as well as those of the mediator's primary profession, and
- 20 hours of continuing education every 2 years in topics related to family mediation.

A postgraduate student enrolled in a state or federally accredited educational institution in the discipline of law, psychiatry, psychology, counseling, family therapy, or any comparable behavioral or social science field may mediate with direct and actual supervision by a qualified mediator.

Rhode Island

There are no state requirements for the practice of mediation.

Rhode Island provides confidentiality for communications with mediators only if the mediator has the following qualifications:

- 30 hours of training, and
- 2 years of professional experience as a mediator or an appointment to mediate given by a judicial or governmental body.

The chief judge's Office of the Family Courts maintains a roster of mediators for divorce mediation. Mediators on the roster meet the above requirements for confidentiality. In addition, most have either a postgraduate degree in mental health or a law degree, and have also taken specialized training in divorce mediation.

South Carolina

There are no state requirements for the practice of mediation.
Qualifications for circuit court mediation include

- being admitted to practice law in South Carolina for at least 3 years,
- being a member in good standing of the South Carolina Bar, and
- not being disbarred, suspended from practicing law, or publicly reprimanded within the last 5 years,

or

- being admitted to practice law in the highest court of another state or the District of Columbia for 3 years,
- holding a law degree from an approved law school,
- being a member in good standing in each jurisdiction where admitted,
- not being disbarred, suspended from practicing law, or publicly reprimanded within the last 5 years,
- being an associate member of the South Carolina Bar in good standing,
- agreeing to be subject to the Rules of Professional Conduct,
- 40 hours of approved civil mediation training,
- demonstrated familiarity with South Carolina mediated settlement conferences,
- being at least 21 years of age,
- good moral character, and
- agreeing to provide mediation to indigents without pay.

Qualifications for family court mediation include

- being a member in good standing of the South Carolina Bar, *or*

- being admitted to practice law in the highest court of another state or the District of Columbia,
- holding a law degree from an approved law school,
- being a member in good standing in each jurisdiction where admitted,
- not being disbarred, suspended from practicing law, or publicly reprimanded within the last 5 years,
- being an associate member of the South Carolina bar in good standing, and
- agreeing to be subject to the Rules of Professional Conduct,

or

- being a licensed psychologist, a licensed master social worker, a licensed professional counselor, a licensed marital and family therapist, or a licensed physician specializing in psychiatry,
- 40 hours of approved family court mediation training,
- a demonstration of familiarity with South Carolina mediated settlement conferences,
- being at least 21 years of age,
- good moral character,
- not having, within the last 5 years, been denied a professional license or disciplined, and
- agreeing to provide mediation to indigents without pay.

South Dakota

There are no state requirements for the practice of mediation.

Qualifications for court-appointed mediation in family courts, include

- 40 hours of training and consultation with an experienced mediator for at least three mediation sessions; or 5 years of experience in mediating custody and visitation issues, with a minimum of 20 mediations during that period,
- knowledge of the South Dakota court system and procedures in contested family matters,
- knowledge of South Dakota family law as applied to custody and visitation issues,

- knowledge of child development and the impact of divorce or separation,
- knowledge of available resources,
- knowledge of interviewing and mediation techniques applicable to the family setting, and
- continuing education courses.

Tennessee

There are no state requirements for the practice of mediation. The ADR Commission maintains a list of family mediators and a list of general-civil mediators. Court-ordered mediation and court-annexed programs must use mediators from these lists. The parties are free to choose other than listed mediators.

Qualifications to be listed as a general-civil mediator include

- a bachelor's degree in any field and 6 years of practice, or a master's degree in any field and 4 years of practice,
- 40 hours of approved training with specified components,
- observing one mediation conducted by a listed mediator,
- a willingness to undertake mentorship and pro bono obligations,
- good moral character,
- adherence to the Standards of Professional Conduct, and
- 6 hours of continuing education every 2 years.

Qualifications to be listed as a family mediator include

- a CPA license or a graduate degree,
- 4 years of experience in psychiatry, psychology, counseling, social work, education, law, or accounting,
- 40 hours of family mediation training with specified components including domestic violence mediation,
- 6 hours of training in Tennessee family law and court procedure,
- a willingness to undertake mentorship and pro bono obligations,

- good moral character,
- adherence to the Standards of Professional Conduct, and
- 6 hours of continuing education every 2 years.

Texas

There are no state requirements for the practice of mediation.

An impartial third party appointed for dispute resolution services by a court or a governmental body must have 40 classroom hours of approved training in dispute resolution techniques. For parent–child disputes, an additional 24 hours of training in the fields of family dynamics, child development, and family law is required.

In appropriate circumstances, a court may appoint a person as an impartial third party who does not qualify as described above if the appointment is based on legal or other professional training or experience in particular dispute resolution processes.

Utah

There are no state requirements for the practice of mediation. The Administrative Office of the Courts maintains the court-annexed alternative dispute resolution program roster of mediators, for public information and quality assurance. Qualifications to be included on this list include completing 30 hours of training in mediation and having mediated three cases or 10 hours. Parties are free to choose a mediator not on the roster.

Vermont

There are no state requirements for the practice of mediation.

The Vermont Family Court Mediation Program has defined criteria for their list of contracted mediators, including completing

- 100 hours of training: 28 hours of basic and 72 hours in divorce mediation with specified components,

- ▶ 40 hours of mediation experience, with 30 hours as an intern divorce mediator and 5 hours of supervision between the intern mediator and the supervising mediator, and
- ▶ 20 hours of continuing education every 2 years.

Virginia

There are no state requirements for the practice of mediation.

Qualifications of court-referred mediators for General District Court include

- ▶ having a bachelor's degree or equivalent,
- ▶ completing 20 hours of certified training,
- ▶ observation of two complete cases or 8 additional hours of training,
- ▶ supervised comediation of three cases or 5 hours with written evaluation and recommendation from a certified mentor,
- ▶ completing 4 hours of certified training in the Virginia judicial system or equivalent experience, and
- ▶ adhering to ethical standards.

Qualifications of court-referred mediators for juvenile and domestic relations district court include

- ▶ having a bachelor's degree or equivalent,
- ▶ completing 40 hours of certified training,
- ▶ observation of two complete cases or 8 additional hours of training,
- ▶ supervised comediation of five cases or 10 hours with written evaluation and recommendation from a certified mentor,
- ▶ completing 4 hours of certified training in the Virginia judicial system or equivalent experience, and
- ▶ adhering to ethical standards.

Qualifications of court-referred mediators for circuit court-civil mediation include

- ▶ having a bachelor's degree or equivalent,
- ▶ completing 40 hours of certified training including 20 in family mediation,

Credentialing and Training

- observation of two complete cases or 8 additional hours of training,
- supervised comediation of five cases or 10 hours with written evaluation and recommendation from a certified mentor,
- completing 4 hours of certified training in the Virginia judicial system or equivalent experience, and
- adhering to ethical standards.

Qualifications of court-referred mediators for circuit court-family mediation include

- having a bachelor's degree or equivalent,
- completing 52 hours of certified training with specified components,
- observation of two complete cases or 8 additional hours of training,
- supervised comediation of five cases or 10 hours with written evaluation and recommendation from a certified mentor,
- completing 4 hours of certified training in the Virginia judicial system or equivalent experience, and
- adhering to ethical standards.

Washington

There are no state requirements for the practice of mediation.

Qualifications required to be registered as a mediator for malpractice cases include

- being an attorney,
- having been a member of the Washington State Bar Association for at least 5 years,
- having experience or expertise related to litigating actions arising from injury occurring as a result of healthcare,
- having 6 hours of continuing legal education mediator training,
- having acted as a mediator in at least 10 cases, 3 of which were medical malpractice,

or

- being a retired judge having experience or expertise related to actions arising from injury occurring as a result of healthcare, as well as satisfying the requirements above.

West Virginia

There are no state requirements for the practice of mediation. Qualifications include

- having a 4-year degree from an accredited college or university,
- completing a 40-hour approved domestic relations course,
- two observations of family court mediations,
- three comediations with experienced family court mediators,
- possessing professional liability insurance, and
- agreeing to complete 12 hours of family court mediator continuing education every 2 years.

Wisconsin

There are no state requirements for the practice of mediation. The only statewide mediation program is the Medical Mediation Panel. Medical malpractice cases are required by statute to be mediated by a three-person panel consisting of an attorney, a doctor, and one of a list of lay persons appointed by the governor. No mediation training or experience is required. The Medical Mediation Panels coordinator generally selects an attorney with mediation experience and a doctor with substantive experience in the type of case being mediated.

Wyoming

There are no state requirements for the practice of mediation. The State Court Administrator keeps a statewide roster of qualified mediators. Mediators must present documented evidence of training in their specific area.

MEDIATION TRAINING 101

The most general type of mediation training you can get is basic training. There are many places you can go for basic training. For example, you might look into the many mediation centers in your community. These centers are nonprofit, state-funded facilities that provide mediation services to members of the community. They are mainly volunteer-based. Through community centers you can get training at a relatively low price, certainly significantly lower than what is available through private mediation groups. There are some disadvantages associated with these centers. Typically, the trainers may not be as experienced or credentialed as you might like; they might be someone who has taken that center's mediation course and does not have the amount of experience in the field you might prefer.

Another option is to go through a private accreditation association. Such programs are more expensive than those offered at the community mediation centers, but you benefit by having access to the curriculum and information regarding the educators before you pay for the program.

Regardless of which option you choose, you can expect that you will be spending 25 to 40 hours in a classroom setting. Any good training program will focus on communication and listening skills. Most curriculums will include the rules of a mediation, the importance of impartiality and confidentiality, the psychology of human conflict, ethical standards in mediation, and listening and communication techniques as well as negotiation theory. Here are some common topics:

- overview of ADR processes
- principles of mediation
- stages and goals of the mediation process
- the role of the mediator
- the nature of conflict and behaviors in conflict
- mediation skills, including negotiation skills, interactive listening, question asking, use of neutral language, reframing, interest identification, addressing barriers to agreement, and agreement writing
- values and bias awareness
- cultural diversity
- power imbalance
- working with attorneys and representatives of parties
- ethical issues, including confidentiality, impartiality, informed consent, conflict of interest, fees, responsibilities to third parties, advertising and soliciting, and withdrawal by the mediator

BEFORE YOU SIGN UP FOR A MEDIATION TRAINING PROGRAM

- Make sure it meets any requirements or qualification standards in the state you are looking to practice.
- Make sure it is aligned with your philosophy. There are different mediation styles and ideologies with which to mediate; you should understand and like what your program proposes.
- Make sure the lead trainer of the program can tell you what kind of techniques and skills the program will be proposing as integral to your practice.
- Make sure the lead trainer is knowledgeable and experienced.
- Make sure you know the student-to-teacher ratio.
- Make sure you enjoy the format of the program. Is it mainly lectures or role-play, for instance?

If you choose to specialize, you can get mediation training that is more specific to your niche. This is especially true if you are looking to mediate family matters. This niche often has more stringent requirements because of the sensitive nature of the specialty.

You can also get mediation training and credentialing through colleges and universities. As mediation is growing in popularity, many institutions are offering everything from individual courses to credentialing courses. Even entire degrees in conflict resolution are available.

There are many routes you can go to get the training that will best help you succeed. You would be hard-pressed to find a mediator who thinks training is unnecessary, but what kind of training you get and where you go for training depends on your budget and your interest. Be diligent about it; do your research and make sure you pick a program that will be both enjoyable and beneficial.

SAMPLE MEDIATION CERTIFICATION COURSE

Foundation Course

Mediation Training Institute International (MTI) takes pride in providing the most intensive, comprehensive, and effective mediator certification training available anywhere—

Credentialing and Training

hence, we are the recognized global leader in mediator training and certification. Learners may expect to work hard, but will complete the training prepared to function successfully as professional mediators, whether internally within their employing organizations or externally with clients.

The mediation model learned in MTI's training was developed by the PULSE Institute, hence the references to PULSE in the outline below.

Please note: *The following is a typical schedule. Selection, sequence, emphasis, and timing of program components and instructional activities may be adjusted to meet the needs of participants as they learn.*

DAY ONE

8:00 Check in, receive resource materials

8:30 PULSE Concepts: Learn and understand the PULSE Frame for mediated conversations. PULSE Concepts is a thorough introduction to a comprehensive, coherent communication skill set which will enable you to become an effective mediator.

Module 1: Prepare for the Learning—How Will the Learning be Structured?

- Course purpose
- Course process
- Course protocol and introductions
- Course goals and objectives

9:30 Break (estimated)

10:15 Module 2: Uncover the PULSE Frame—What is Mediation?

- Jigsaw reading activity: *PULSE Conversations for Change*, by Nancy Love
- Video: *The PULSE Mediated Conversation*

12:00 Lunch

1:15 Module 3: Uncover PULSE Process—How Does Mediation Work?

- Three aspects of communication and conversation
- Forces at work in conversation, from *Managing Differences*, by Dan Dana
- Cycles of perception

2:45 Break (estimated)

3:00 Module 4: Uncover PULSE Response with the Enneagram—Why Does Mediation Work?

- Body, head, and heart types
- Conflict styles: The conflict continuum

5:00 Conclude Day One

DAY TWO

8:00 Module 5: Uncover PULSE Content — How Do Mediators Think?

- Assumptions of PULSE Mediated Conversations: The influence of appreciative inquiry
- The ladder of inference: Unraveling perceptions
- The process and frame for mediation: A dynamic conversation
- The Script for Mediation

9:45 Break (estimated)

10:00 Factors to consider in mediation: When is it appropriate?

12:00 Lunch

1:15 Module 6: Learn Skills for Changing Perceptions

- *Gone* exercise: Self-awareness in listening
- GHOST: A protocol for effective speaking and listening
- HEART: Skills for reflective listening
- POWER: Skills for active listening
- Stay the course: Five skills to steer the conversation

2:30 Break (estimated)

2:45

- PULSE language skills activity: A presentation of skills
- Connecting skills and the Enneagram: Body, head, and heart language
- Video: *The Art of Active Listening*

5:00 Conclude Day Two

DAY THREE

8:00 PULSE Mediation Practice: PULSE Practice is the opportunity to learn through practice each stage of the PULSE Mediated Conversations Frame. You will gain an understanding of the intention of each stage of the PULSE Frame and the confidence to use the skills immediately.

Module 1: Prepare for the Learning—How Will the Practice Proceed?

- Purpose, process, protocol
- Uncover what is known about the PULSE Frame

GHOST, HEART, POWER: review the skills for effective speaking and listening

9:30 Break (estimated)

9:45 Module 2: Learn How to Prepare for the Mediated Conversation through Practice

- How will the conversation proceed?
- The conversation map: Prepare—who is talking to whom?
- PULSE CPR: Content process, response for the Prepare Stage
- Practice Prepare in groups with coaches

Credentialing and Training

12:00 Lunch

1:15 Module 3: Learn How to Uncover the Circumstance through Practice

- What is the circumstance?
- The conversation map: Uncover—Who is talking to whom?
- PULSE CPR: Content, process, response for the Uncover Stage
- Practice Uncover in groups with coaches

2:45 Break (estimated)

3:00 Module 4: Learn How to Use the POWER tool to Reframe through Practice

- TAXI exercise: Practicing the skills for effective speaking and listening

5:00 Conclude Day Three

DAY FOUR

8:00 Module 5: Learn How to Learn the Significance and Identify Criteria for Resolution through Practice

- Why is the circumstance significant? Where is the rub?
- Shifting from positions to criteria: Identifying criteria for a better future
- Using a summary goal statement
- The conversation map: Learn—who is talking to whom?
- PULSE CPR for the Learn Stage

10:00 Break (estimated)

10:15 Practice Learn in groups with coaches

12:15 Lunch

1:30 Module 6: Learn How to Search and Explain through Practice

- What If and What Next?
- Brainstorm activity

2:45 Break (estimated)

3:00

- Writing the plan activity
- The conversation map: Search and Explain—who is talking to whom?
- PULSE CPR in Search and Explain

5:00 Conclude Day Four

DAY FIVE

8:00 Module 7: Putting it all together

- Practice Prepare, Uncover, Learn, Search, and Explain in groups with coaches
- Debrief in large group with coaches

12:00 Lunch and breaks for Day Five will be at the discretion of groups and coaches

1:15 Module 8: Search Applications for the PULSE Conversation
- Explain in writing a plan of action based on the learning

3:30 Groups reconvene at 3:30 for debrief and final activities

5:00 Program concludes

Source: Mediation Training Institute International

SAMPLE DIVORCE MEDIATION COURSE

This Divorce Mediation Training sample course represents a 40-hour, five-day course. Suitable for the beginner, the seasoned practitioner, or the layman who is interested in exploring what mediation has to offer, this course has been designed to provide participants with the tools and techniques necessary to be a successful mediator.

Classes are small in order to maintain a lively, interactive environment. The instructor will focus on the skills participants need as a mediator, and the participant will have the chance to practice putting the skills to use.

DAY ONE
- Mediation Definition
- Divorce Mediation Steps
- Basic Mediator Skills
- Basic Role-Play Facts
- Mediation Structure
- Checklist of Issues

Mediation Materials: *Healy, Fiske, Richmond & Matthew*
- Introductory Packet, with Contract
- Intake Form
- Homework

Mediation Materials: *Diane Neumann & Associates*
- Introductory Packet
- Contract
- Information Form
- Massachusetts Custody Statute, c. 208 sec. 31
- Maine Parenting Statute, title 19 sec. 792
- *Cooperative Parenting Plans*, Massachusetts Bar Association
- Haynes, John: *Shared Parenting Case Study*

DAY TWO
- Psychological Stages of Divorce
- Mayer, Bernard: *The Dynamics of Conflict*, Chapter 6
- Child Support Outline
- Massachusetts Child Support Guidelines
- Standard of Living Analysis

DAY THREE
- Marital Home
- Property Division Outline
- Massachusetts Property Division Statute, c. 208 sec. 34 (includes alimony)
- Maine Property Division Statute, title 19 sec. 722-A

DAY FOUR
- Sample Memorandum of Understanding
- Sample Separation Agreement
- Neumann, Dianne: *Power Imbalance*
- Cycle of Violence
- Tolman Screening Model
- Johnston & Campbell: *Domestic Violence in Families*
- Alimony: Brief Summary

DAY FIVE
- Grebe, Sarah: *Family Mediation and Family Therapy*
- Ethical Opinion, Massachusetts Bar Association
- Massachusetts Mediation Confidentiality Statute, c. 223 sec. 23C
- New Hampshire Mediation Statute, c. 328-C
- Maine Mediation Statute, title 19 sec. 636
- *Standards of Practice*, Massachusetts Council on Family Mediation
- *Standards of Practice*, Association for Conflict Resolution
- *Certification Requirements*, Massachusetts Council on Family Mediation
- *Uniform Rules on Dispute Resolution*, Massachusetts Supreme Judicial Court

General Materials
- Ury & Fisher, excerpt from *Getting to Yes*
- Folger & Baruch Bush, *Transformative Mediation*
- Dworkin & London, *What is a Fair Agreement?*

Becoming a LEGAL MEDIATOR

- Fiske, John A., Mediation Chapter, *MCLE Family Law Manual*
- Moore, Christopher, *The Mediation Process*, Chapters 1 & 2
- Bibliography

Source: Divorce Mediation Training

SAMPLE CERTIFICATE PROGRAM

NYU School of Continuing and Professional Studies

Certificate in Conflict and Dispute Resolution

Professionals in almost every sector of today's business world benefit greatly from enhancing their skills in dispute resolution. This certificate is a hands-on training program in the various methods of negotiation, mediation, and arbitration.

Upon completion of the program, students will be well versed in the following:

- theory, practice, and limitations of the negotiation and arbitration process
- role of third-party intervention in the resolution of conflicts, focusing on the role of the mediator as facilitator

This certificate is awarded to students who successfully complete five courses—three required and two electives.

THE INSIDE TRACK

SHELLEY ROSSOFF OLSEN, ESQ.
FORMER SENIOR COURT MEDIATOR
SUMMARY JUDGE TRIAL JUDGE, NEW YORK
NATIONAL ARBITRATION AND MEDIATION (NAM)

I think mediation training can sometimes be a waste of time. I wouldn't mind taking a course, in fact there's one at Pepperdine happening this summer I'm interested in. But, attorneys have to complete CLE, or continuing legal education, credits regularly and many of them spend the time, you know, not really paying attention, making shopping lists, thinking about other things. So, although CLE credits are mandatory, I don't know how much good they do.

On the other hand, there was a time when not having formal training really hurt me. I was being interviewed for a judiciary job for the mayor's office. I was one of the last three in the interview process and at that point you get interviewed by a panel. At the end of the interview, they critique your interview. So, after my interview, I was told that the panel didn't really understand what it was that I did. I suppose if I had had some formal training, I would have been able to talk about mediation techniques or use some formal language that they could understand. I guess, just being a really good mediator without the formal information didn't really work in that case. In the end, I didn't get that job.

CHAPTER six

HOW TO FIND YOUR FIRST JOB

Starting the hunt for your first job in a new field can be daunting. Especially if you are completely new to the legal profession, you may need some help identifying the places to begin and the ways to approach people. Every profession has its little quirks and tweaks; this chapter shows you what you can do to make finding your first job a little easier.

If you are going the independent route—setting up a practice as an independent mediator—you have to be prepared to do relentless marketing. Unfortunately, many of the people who want to get into the business don't want to do relentless marketing. But that is the reality of the field.
—Peter Lovenheim

HUNTING FOR a job usually involves three phases: You need to decide whom you are going to contact, you have to advertise yourself, and you have to sell yourself. Deciding whom to contact entails identifying potential employers and narrowing the field to those you think you would most like to work for and those most apt to hire you. Advertising yourself includes writing and sending out resumes and cover letters, but also networking and other methods of bringing your skills to the attention of the right people. Finally, selling yourself involves sitting down face to face with the person who has the authority to hire you and convincing that person you are right for the job.

INTERNSHIPS AND PRACTICUMS

Not only do internships give you valuable experience for your resume, but they can often turn into permanent jobs. An internship provides an opportunity for you to get a look at an employer and for the employer to get a look at you with very little obligation. However, if everybody likes what they see, it is to everyone's benefit to hire a former intern for a permanent position. Keeping in mind that many internships turn into permanent jobs, choose an internship in the genre of work you think you want to be doing for the next several years.

Employers tend to hire mediators with job experience before they hire the most educated or credentialed mediator, so an internship is one way for you to get far ahead of your competition. The more mediation training you have had, whether paid or unpaid, the more desirable you will be to an employer.

One easy way to gain some on-the-job training is to volunteer through the mediation training center where you got your training. Mediation training centers often have some possibilities for volunteering in small-claims cases at local district courts. Experienced mediators work with newly trained mediators to develop their skills, work on their mediation styles, and help with whatever coaching is required. Most of the time it costs nothing to participate in a volunteer program, but sometimes there might be a cost.

Another option for gaining experience is a practicum. A practicum is the practical portion of your mediation studies. In a practicum, you have the opportunity to apply what you learned in your mediation course at a job site under the supervision of practicing mediators. Many mediation centers offer this option to recent graduates of their training programs. The advantages of a practicum include intensive supervision by extremely qualified mediators, coaching for newly trained mediators and graduates of meditation programs, the ability to increase a mediator's effectiveness, and the ability to coach mediators on their skills, mediation style, and negotiation techniques. Unfortunately, there are often space limitations and relatively high costs associated with a practicum.

SAMPLE INTERNSHIP POSTING

You Can Make a Difference as an Intern with the County of Orange

Internship Position Description

Position Title: Conflict Mediation Internship (unpaid internship)

Name and Location of Agency/Department Requesting Intern:

Orange County Human Relations Commission

1300 South Grand Avenue, Bldg. B

Santa Ana, CA 92705

Functions of Agency/Department

The Orange County Human Relations Commission and Council provide programs to foster mutual understanding and respect among residents in order to make Orange County a better place for all people to live, work, and do business. We strive to create a future where our county's diversity is realized as a source of our strength and build bridges of understanding to make our community a place where all people are valued and included.

Intern Duties/Responsibilities

- Perform casework as a mediator in a court-based office (small-claims, debt collection, and unlawful detainers) and/or with community disputes (landlord–tenant, neighbor–neighbor, consumer–merchant, employer–employee, etc.)
- Assist with mediation trainings and presentations
- Assist with community outreach
- Help coordinate and manage volunteer program
- Assist with grant-related documentation and record keeping

Educational Requirements

This internship is appropriate for students or recent graduates with majors in any of the following fields: peace studies, communications, criminal justice, law, human services, social work, psychology, social ecology, political science, public administration, international studies, ethnic studies, or related fields.

Skills, Training or Qualifications

- Bilingual (English-Spanish) language skills are preferred
- Good oral and written communication skills

Interns will be working in a human relations environment and will be expected to deal tactfully and respectfully with sensitive issues involving divergent viewpoints and cultures.

Time Commitment

Interns are required to schedule 8 to 10 hours per week for a minimum of 120 hours. Hours may be scheduled Monday through Friday between 8:00 A.M. and 5:00 P.M. Interns are expected to work a 3- or 4-hour shift, mornings or afternoons. Summer internships are available.

In addition to the required hours mentioned above, interns must complete a 32-hour mediation certification training (unless already trained). A $165 fully refundable deposit is required for training. The fee is refunded and certification is issued upon completion of the internship.

Benefits Available to Intern

As community mediators, interns will develop mediation and negotiation skills and gain practical experience. This is a unique opportunity to work with diverse groups and individuals to promote cooperative and amicable resolution of conflicts. Interns will also have the opportunity to assist with program development and implementation which may include public speaking.

Application Process

E-mail resume and cover letter to the contact listed below. The cover letter is an opportunity for applicants to describe career and academic goals, to elaborate upon personal and academic accomplishments, to share areas of interest that relate to the internship, and to identify what type of internship experience they are seeking. Please include GPA, preferred start and end dates for the internship, number of hours that can be scheduled on a weekly basis, and days/timeframes available to schedule internship hours.

As you have learned, legal mediation is a highly desirable field. There are no federally mandated educational requirements, you can make use of your already existing skills and expertise, and it is a growing industry. Once you are ready to enter the field, however, you will meet some stiff competition for jobs from other applicants. So how do you beat out the competition and get that dream mediation job?

> **SAMPLE MEDIATION APPRENTICESHIP**
>
> *Continuing Education: Accounting, Taxation, and Legal Programs*
>
> In this class, students meet weekly in one of New York City's small-claims courts (evening sessions) to mediate cases referred by the court. Using a comediation model, students work with a mentor to learn the practical skills a mediator needs to resolve cases. After an initial experience comediating with a mentor, students conduct the entire mediation (with your mentor as an observer), including drafting any stipulations the parties may agree to that resolves their case. Students must make a commitment to attend all mediation sessions and are required to maintain a log of cases mediated. Each session includes one hour of discussion, critiquing, and skill-building, followed by two hours of real-time mediation.

WHAT EMPLOYERS LOOK FOR

What are the skills and qualifications a potential employer will be looking for? Regardless of where you look for work as a mediator, you will start to see some commonalities in what mediation employers will recognize as desirable skills.

Education

If your educational background has been in law you will find yourself extremely hirable as a mediator. However, because of the versatility of the field, you can use your educational background, regardless of what it is, to maximize your potential as a candidate. This is especially true if you look for a job within your already established specialty.

If you are looking to work within the court system, you will have to meet relatively stringent educational requirements. Often you will need a bachelor's degree at minimum, including some pretty extensive training and licensing as a mediator. If you are looking for a mediation job in a community mediation center or a private mediation group, however, the educational requirements are much less intense.

Becoming a LEGAL MEDIATOR

BECOMING A FAMILY MEDIATOR

One of the most difficult mediation specializations to get into is family matters. Because of the highly emotional nature of these cases, their complexity, and the multiple parties involved, most employers will require a great deal more experience before you can mediate these cases. If you are interested in this field, a legal background, though helpful, is not mandatory. A background in social work, counseling, or education can also help you gain access to the field.

What you do need—more than anything else—is practical experience. Preferably practical experience includes working with families or at the very least, other types of mediation or conflict management experience, whether paid or unpaid. You can gain valuable practical experience in family matters by volunteering with families in child contact centers, family support centers, or counseling services. Another great way to get some experience is to volunteer at your local community mediation center, especially if they oversee family cases.

If you want to become a family mediator there are several ways to get started. You can apply for a trainee position with a mediation group that specializes in family matters. Or you can pay for training on your own or volunteer, and then apply for jobs after you have had some experience. Either way, most employers will require that you hold some kind of degree or certificate in mediation, and they will want to make sure that you have the right interpersonal skills to handle these very sensitive cases.

Training, Licensing, and Credentialing

Regardless of your educational background, one factor that potential employers will look for is what you have in the way of training, licensing, or credentialing in the field of mediation or conflict resolution. Remember: you are up against many other applicants. The amount of training and credentialing you have will strongly weigh in on an employer's decision. One way to get training is to apply for apprenticeships and internships, discussed earlier in this chapter.

Experience

You already know that you can bring your life experiences and previous work experience with you into your new career as a mediator. Make sure you emphasize how you have acted as a mediator in your life or your previous career. Maybe you have played a part in resolving conflicts in your workplace as a supervisor or a human resource staff member. Maybe you have helped bridge differences on committees or boards or negotiated resolutions among peers. These are all indications that you have what it takes to succeed as a mediator.

Interpersonal Skills

Besides your educational accomplishments and your work history, a potential employer will also look at your interpersonal skills. Interpersonal skills are your capabilities when interacting with others. You may hear interpersonal skills referred to as *people skills* or *communication skills* but they really embrace to a wide range of abilities. The following is a list of the skills a potential employer will look for in a mediator.

Listening and Communication Skills
Listening and communication are probably the most important skills a potential employer will be looking for. You will need to demonstrate your ability to listen actively and to listen to what is being said as well as listening for what is not being said. You will also need to demonstrate that you have impeccable communication skills and that you can effectively articulate to the opposing parties what their individual needs are and help guide them toward a workable solution.

The Ability to Empathize
In mediations, people come to you with a conflict that is causing them pain. A potential employer must be confident that you will approach people with respect and empathy so that you can best guide them to a solution that will relieve them of their pain.

The Ability to Be Attentive
Most people who are attempting to resolve a conflict want to be heard. Often the complaint you hear about the court system is that disputants do not feel that the judge or even their own attorneys are particularly interested in

paying attention to them. As a mediator you will find that you can defuse much anger by simply allowing people to feel heard and heeded. A potential employer will look for a candidate who is able stay focused and is not easily distracted.

The Ability to Be Firm

In mediations, disputants will often try to move the dialogue away from the matter at hand and rehash the issues that led to the conflict. They may also be more interested in blaming the other party or getting defensive than in finding some kind of resolution to the matter. As the mediator, it is your job to guide the mediation effectively in the direction it needs to go in order to be efficient. An employer will look for a candidate who is able to be respectful and polite while maintaining firm control of a stressful situation.

CONDUCTING YOUR JOB SEARCH

Before you look for a job, you need to know the specific kind of job you are looking for. Rather than mediation in general, you might have a specialty in mind, such as personal injury or employer–employees matters. Or you might want to be a mediator in a mediation group or an in-house mediator in a corporation or for the courts.

Look for your dream job right from the start, of course. But be realistic: It is unlikely that you will be hired right out of mediator school to run a mediation group or to supervise several more experienced meditors. Still, it is worth spending some time pursuing the kind of job you think you would love.

If you are in a mediation program, you should definitely get to know the placement director. This is the person whose job it is to help you find a job when you graduate. A good placement office has directories of mediation groups and other businesses in the local area, information about job fairs, and copies of any industry publications that list mediation job openings. A top placement director also maintains contacts with the legal and business communities so that your school's placement office will be one of the first places to hear about a job opening in addition to giving you valuable general information about the market in your area.

Classified Ads

Conventional job hunting wisdom says you should not depend too much on want ads for finding a job. True, you should not depend on them totally, but there do seem to be quite a few mediation jobs advertised in the newspaper. For one thing, many businesses are looking for human resource specialists or other administrators to serve as in-house conflict resolution experts. Such a job may not be listed as a mediator position but it may be a great way to get your foot in the door. And even if you do not find a job through the classifieds, you can learn quite a lot about the market in your area. If you start paying attention to the ads well before you are done with your training, you will be able to start a list of the places that hire mediators and other conflict resolution professionals.

The classifieds can yield other useful information, such as typical salaries and benefits in your area. One of the hardest questions to answer on an application or in an interview is *What is your desired salary?* If you have been watching the ads, you will have an idea of the going rate. You can also get information about temporary and part-time jobs. In some areas, temporary and part-time jobs may be a common way for mediators to begin their careers.

Online Resources

These days, the Internet is changing and growing so fast that there is little point in directing you to specific sites; they could easily be gone by the time you read this. But the major employment sites listed under that heading are likely to be around for a while. By the way, it is always worthwhile to start with your favorite search engine (such as Yahoo! or Google) to look for these and other employment sites.

What is true of classified advertisements is also true of the Web. You may happen on a job opening that is right for you, but there is also a wealth of information. Many websites contain legal and conflict resolution information; you should spend some time early in your career visiting some of these areas. You can learn about salaries, job frustrations and pleasures, and various specialties that you may not have thought of, and you can even do some cyber-networking.

Another great online resource is the employment section of mediation groups and other conflict resolution websites. An easy way to find these sites is simply to search for *mediation groups*, *conflict resolution*, or *dispute resolution* in the keyword search of your favorite search engine. Some examples are:

International Crisis Group (www.crisisgroup.org)
National Arbitration and Mediation (www.namadr.com/careers.cfm)
JAMS Arbitration, Mediation and ADR Services (www.jamsadr.com/careers)
American Arbitration Association (https://apps.adr.org/ecenter)
International Peace and Conflict Resolution (www.american.edu/sis/ipcr)

Employment Sites

Here is a list of employment sites that offer mediation jobs. This index consists of general employment sites that include mediation and other conflict resolution jobs. In some cases, the job openings may not be for a mediator specifically, but the job specifications correspond to the capabilities of a mediator. For example, many human resource job openings require that the applicant be capable of resolving disputes between employees, even though the job classification is not for a mediator per se.

Indeed (www.indeed.com)
Monster (www.monster.com)
America's Job Bank (The Public Employment Service) (www.ajb.dni.us)
Career Builder (www.careerbuilder.com)
Idealist (www.idealist.org)

Networking

Networking is about much more than just meeting people. The point of networking is to use the relationships you have and new ones you make to help you find a job. A successful network continues to grow; it does not die once you get a job. As your network of acquaintances expands—one person leading you to the next and that person leading you to the next—eventually, you will get to the person who is hiring.

Networking is a major job-search tactic used by people in all industries. But no matter how widespread its use, networking remains intimidating to some, who picture it as insincere small talk or handshaking. When properly done, however, networking is completely sincere and can provide many benefits, including

- ▶ mentoring,
- ▶ making contacts within a hiring firm or company,
- ▶ furthering training, and
- ▶ getting information about trends in the industry.

The key to successful networking is to break down the process into easy-to-follow steps, which are reviewed over the next few pages. You will find these steps useful not only in your mediation job search, but also in other areas of your life.

Step One: Identify Small Goals
Of course, your ultimate goal, not only for networking but also for the entire job-search process, is to find a great job. But you should not approach day-to-day networking as a means to that larger goal. Instead, as your first step, identify smaller goals that can be met quickly. For instance, let us say you have narrowed down your search to three mediation groups in your area. Now you want to get inside information about these groups to decide with which one to apply for a job. Or, you may simply be seeking advice from those already working in the field. Once your goals are identified, you can best determine how to meet them.

Step Two: Be Informed
If your goal is to seek advice about family mediation in your area, get as much information as you can first. Research the mediation groups that hire family mediators. Understand the mediation field in general, too. You want to sound like you have done your homework when you begin to make contacts.

This is also the step in which you begin to make a list of potential contacts that may help you meet your goals. If you are in school, the person at the job placement office should be at the head of your list. Next, compile a list of the mediators working in your area; they would also make great networking contacts. Finally, see if you can add the names of the people in charge of hiring at various mediation companies or the owners of the companies. The students and teachers you met during your training are also good candidates for this list.

Step Three: Make a Connection
Using the list of potential contacts you developed in step two, build a network of mediators who work at the offices you are interested in joining. Call them, or visit their offices. Even if they are busy, most people like to talk about themselves and their jobs. They themselves were once new to the field, so if you are careful not to take up too much of their time, they will probably be glad to give you some information. Begin by introducing yourself, showing that you are informed (step two) and interested in what they have to say.

Step Four: Ask for What You Want
If your contact indicates a willingness to help you, be honest and direct about what you want. If your goal is to find out inside information about the office in which a contact works, tell him or her that you are thinking of applying to work there. Then ask such questions as

> *How do you like the office?*
> *What are the benefits of working here?*
> *What is the office atmosphere like?*
> *Where else have you worked, and how does this office compare?*

Sending a thank you note to someone who helps you is a nice touch that makes you stand out in that person's mind.

Step Five: Expand Your Network
One of the most valuable pieces of information you can get from a contact is another contact. After getting the information you need to meet your step

one goals, simply ask if your contact would mind sharing with you the name of another person who might also be able to help you.

Also consider requesting informational interviews at companies that interest you. An informational interview is one in which you meet with someone to find out about the company. Such an interview may be an excellent opportunity to

- ▶ learn more about how the firm works,
- ▶ gain interview experience, and
- ▶ make a contact that might help you get a job in the future.

You can also expand your circle of contacts by joining professional organizations while you are still a student. Both the ACR and MBB offer discounted student memberships; most other professional organizations do so as well. Be sure to join both national organizations and their local chapters. Although the national organizations can give you valuable information, it is on the local level that you will accomplish more of your networking goals. Go to local meetings and ask questions—remind people that you are a student and a soon-to-be job hunter—and volunteer for committees. The members of your local mediation association will most likely know about job openings before anyone else does.

Step Six: Organize Yourself

You have probably already written down your goals and made lists of contacts. Once you have spoken with some of your contacts, organization becomes even more important. You will need to keep track of the contacts and the information you receive from them. Whenever you need to connect with this person again, you will be able to access your information easily. There are software packages that can help you keep track of your networking contacts, or you can simply use a notebook and organize them yourself.

For each contact, make a note of the following information:

name
address
e-mail address
phone number (work, pager, cellular phone, residence)

fax number
company name
job title
first meeting—where, when, the topics you discussed
most recent contact—when, why, and how

Step Seven: Maintain Your Contacts

It is important to maintain your contacts once you have established them. Try to reach people again within a couple of weeks of meeting them. You can send a note of thanks, ask a question, or send a piece of information related to your conversation with them. This contact cements your meeting in their minds, so they will remember you more readily when you call them again in the future. If you have not communicated with your contacts for a few months, you might send them a note or e-mail about an article you read, or about relevant new technology or law, to keep your name fresh in their minds.

As a group, mediators are usually good at networking and supporting one another. It is a good idea to keep a list of mediation groups at which you can get jobs, and share it with mediators you know. Many mediators volunteer, partly to learn and partly to network. Doing volunteer work looks good on your resume and helps you meet people. Some mediators go on to get good jobs through the people they meet during volunteer work.

ALTERNATIVE CAREER OPTIONS

A number of alternative careers besides mediation can utilize your mediation skills.

Ombudsman

An ombudsman is a neutral party who acts as an intermediary between groups of people. Ombudsmen need not hold a law degree, although some legal training is beneficial.

An ombudsman has very similar skills to that of a mediator; the difference between the two is that the ombudsman's main role is to hear complaints and address them within a corporation or in government. An ombudsman's input may change corporate policies or even legislature. Also, an ombudsman typically only works with one party—the party that has felt wronged—although at times he or she may facilitate dialogue between both parties.

An ombudsman is used in a variety of settings: in public agencies, in private businesses, in healthcare companies, in educational institutions—really, anywhere conflicts can arise. In a government setting, it is very important that the ombudsman have no political ties and no political loyalties in order to remain impartial. The goal of the ombudsman is to serve as an intermediary between the public and the government, to help facilitate cross dialogue, and to address complaints that arise between the two parties.

A corporate ombudsman will typically serve as a neutral, third party between employees and the corporation. Because it is the ombudsman's obligation to remain neutral, employees can freely address conflicts and concerns and come up with ways to resolve them. An employee's concern may result in a change in corporate policy because of the ombudsman's intervention.

If you are interested in learning more about becoming an ombudsman, visit the following websites:

International Ombudsman Association (www.ombudsassociation.org)
United States Ombudsman Association (www.usombudsman.org)
The ABA's Ombuds Committee (www.abanet.org)

Mediation Teaching

If you are really an educator at heart, but love mediation and the mediation process, a career in mediation teaching may be for you. As ADR and mediation in particular become more and more mainstream and as more and more people realize the benefits of the field, the demand for mediation teachers has also increased. Today, many undergraduate, postgraduate, and certificate programs are offered at colleges and universities across the country, resulting in a continuing demand for teachers. As a teacher you may choose to offer your services as a practicing mediator part time for a group or even as an in-house mediator for the school where you teach.

> **SAMPLE JOB DESCRIPTION**
>
> **Position:** Assistant Professor of Conflict Resolution.
>
> **Organization:** The dispute resolution section of a private university in Omaha, Nebraska.
>
> **Job Description:** Full-time faculty position in conflict resolution. Responsibilities include teaching graduate courses, serving as an academic advisor to students, aiding in the development of the curriculum, participating in academic research, and participating in community service.
>
> **Skills and Qualifications:** A terminal degree (PhD, JD, or similar); substantial training and experience in dispute resolution (including mediation and other processes); and a background in teaching.

Conflict Resolution Consulting and Coaching

Conflict resolution consulting and coaching are closely related to the mediation field. Both fields require similar skill sets as a mediator but are somewhat different in their applications.

A conflict resolution consultant works within organizations to set up conflict resolution procedures. The types of procedures and policies you would develop as a conflict resolution consultant would depend on the type of organization and industry you were consulting for. For example, you might be responsible for solidifying conflict resolution protocols to be used when employees within an organization are in dispute, or you might be setting up procedures to follow when customers and companies are in conflict. This line of work can be especially suitable for you if you enjoy the dispute resolution process and also enjoy working in business.

ONLINE DISPUTE RESOLUTION

Online Dispute Resolution (ODR) is a newer form of conflict resolution that uses technology and technological advances to resolve disputes between parties. Basically, ODR is what happens when all or most of the ADR process happened online—including the initial filing of a claim, the appointment of a mediator or some other third-party neutral, the collection of evidence and documents, the oral hearing, the online discussions, and even the completion of the final binding settlement agreement. ODR has been used to address many different types of disputes including conflicts arising out of business transactions, e-commerce, and even marital disputes.

There are two main categories of ODR. One is known as *automated negotiation*. This term refers to the method used to determine the amount of money awarded to a party in a dispute. The method works similarly to an auction. The other category is *assisted negotiation*, in which the technology itself assists the negotiation process between the parties. In essence, the technology functions as the mediator.

Until recently, SquareTrade was the leading ODR provider for consumer mediation. It resolved consumer disputes for several online marketplaces such as eBay. SquareTrade handled disputes between sellers and buyers on eBay, either via assisted negotiation or with an actual mediation.

The mediation process via SquareTrade started when a buyer or a seller filed a web-based standard claim form that identified the type of dispute and offered a list of common solutions to choose from. The other party was then contacted via e-mail, was informed about the SquareTrade process, and was invited to participate. The other party filed the response and also chose a resolution from the list. If both parties agreed on the same resolution, the conflict had been resolved. If not, the parties were moved into a mediation-type process. This process utilized software tools to shape communication between the parties into a productive and polite negotiation. The software structured the mediation process by encouraging agreements, setting deadlines, and even changing the tone of the communication exchanged between the parties (www.squaretrade.com/spl/jsp/eby/eb_faq.jsp).

WebMediate, Inc., is a Boston-based company that provides online dispute resolution for claims arising from conflicts between businesses, in e-marketplaces, and from insurance claims. WebMediate's software enables disputants to resolve their disputes quickly, fairly, and confidentially. WebMediate combines web-based technology with a network of nationwide resolution professionals to resolve business disputes as amicably and quickly as possible.

A conflict resolution coach uses mediation skills to work with one individual's ability to handle disputes. A conflict resolution coach teaches others the kind of skills necessary to be good resolvers of conflicts themselves. Conflict resolution coaches often work within organizations. As a conflict resolution coach, you might work with managers on obtaining better tools for dealing with their staff.

THE INSIDE TRACK

JESSICA LEE STOCKTON, ESQ.
VICE PRESIDENT OF COMMUNICATIONS AND DEVELOPMENT
NATIONAL ARBITRATION AND MEDIATION (NAM)

What do I look for when recruiting mediators? Well, first, it is important to remember that clients come back to us because of our mediators. Most of our clients are attorneys. They might think that the parties in a particular case would settle in mediation. Or the case is in litigation and while they're waiting for the court to move the case along, they are trying to get it settled this way. Also, because we rarely, if ever, get parties without an attorney, all of the mediators at NAM are retired judges or lawyers. It is not that I wouldn't hire someone who had no legal expertise; in fact I know of some cases on construction sites where it would be much more helpful to have a mediator who has some real knowledge about that kind of work as opposed to someone who has legal expertise. It is just that it would be difficult for me to sell a nonlegal mediator to our clients since they are all lawyers. I would definitely have a nonlawyer mediator with some specific specialty as a comediator. You know, most of the time just one mediator mediates the case and they might employ the help of an expert. But it is possible to have a comediator. In the kind of cases that we work with here at NAM, the judges can help guide the disputants by telling them what might happen in court in that particular jurisdiction. So, here at NAM, I look for a few different things. Personality, personality, personality. A uniqueness that's going to make people want to come back to that particular mediator. They may be very formal and polite and never upset anyone or they might tell off the attorneys and yell at them—both types are fine as long as there's something great about them and then it is our job to match the right parties and cases with the right mediator. I also look at their expertise and their background—what kind of work they have done in the past or what kinds of cases they have experience with.

CHAPTER seven

JOB-SEARCH SKILLS AND INTERVIEWING

Once you have narrowed your job search and located some job openings, the process of selling yourself to a potential employer or client begins. Your first contact with a potential employer or client may be on paper, in the form of a resume and cover letter. If you make a good impression on paper, your next contact will be in person, in the form of an interview.

You never really understand a person until you consider things from his point of view . . . until you climb into his skin and walk around in it.
—Harper Lee (1926–), *To Kill a Mockingbird*

WHETHER YOU are responding to an advertisement, following up on a networking opportunity, or making a cold contact, your resume is usually the first means by which a potential employer or a potential client learns about you. Your resume is the advertisement you write to help sell yourself, and it helps to think of it that way. Think about newspaper or magazine ads you have seen that made you want to go to a store and look at the item. Maybe you did not end up buying it, but the ad made you consider it. That is what you want a resume to do for you.

A successful advertisement catches your attention by combining several elements: composition, clarity, content, and concentration. Falling short in any of these areas can cause a reader to pass over the ad; you want to make sure that a prospective employer does not do so. There are many sources available to learn about writing resumes; this chapter addresses the specific issue of resumes for legal mediators.

Even if you have written dozens of resumes in your day, it is probably worth your while to find a good book or article on resume writing to help you draft a resume for your new legal mediation career. Books such as *Resumes That Get You Hired* (LearningExpress, 2006) contain excellent general guidelines. And there are plenty of online resources to help you create a winning resume, including the following:

ABA Resume Writing (www.abastaff.com/resources/resume.html)
Accent Resume Writing (www.accent-resume-writing.com)
Creative Professional Resumes (www.resumesbycpr.com)
Free Resume Tips (www.free-resume-tips.com)
Professional Association of Resume Writers (www.parw.com)
Proven Resumes (www.provenresumes.com)
eResumes & Resume Writing Services (www.eresumes.com)
Resumania (www.resumania.com)
Resumedotcom (www.resumedotcom.com)

Once you have a rough draft, consider the four important elements of resume writing.

WHAT YOUR RESUME SHOULD LOOK LIKE

If your resume does not look acceptable on a very basic level, it will probably get no more than a quick glance. You can find all kinds of advice about the length of a resume, the kind of paper it should be on, and what fonts you should use, as well as some suggestions for resumes that are real eye catchers. When looking for a job in the mediation field, keep in mind that although it is an emerging profession, it is closely tied to the fairly conservative, tradition-bound legal profession. In fact, your employers and clients could very well be lawyers, so it may be in your best interest to follow their lead. This does not mean that you cannot find a mediation group where T-shirts are the preferred office attire. What it means is that you need to make sure you look the part. Err on the side of caution, at least at first.

So: make conservative choices when it comes to your resume. Forgo the neon red paper and avoid parchment. Stick with something tried and true, such as white, cream, or gray. Many larger mediation groups will want to scan your resume into their computer system to make it accessible to the several people in the group who are part of the hiring process. Employment agencies will want to do this, too. To help with the scanning process, send out originals of your resume, not photocopies. Light-colored, 8.5 × 11 paper, printed on one side only, will scan more easily. Try to avoid using tabs and any graphics or shadings. Do not use vertical or horizontal lines. Finally, Do not staple the pages of your resume together. If your resume is fairly conservative, it should scan fine. There is more information on computers and resumes in the next section.

Do not use an off-the-wall font. Would you want to read this whole page if it were printed like this?

Stick to more common computer fonts, such as Times New Roman. Ignore advice on how to make your resume stand out from all the rest. Especially avoid composing your resume so that it looks like a pamphlet or a pleading or a court decision. Like many other nontraditional tactics, this would send the message that you have resorted to flashy advertisement because you do not believe you can get an interview on your merits. Mediators and mediation group owners feel the same way about flashy resumes as the rest of us feel about that guy who comes on TV late at night screaming about stereos or used cars and causes us to dive for the remote's mute button.

Some resume advisers will tell you that you should never send out a resume that is more than one page long. This is not necessarily true. If, however, you have prior work experience and you draft a resume that is more than two pages, or you went straight from high school to legal mediator training and you draft a resume that is more than one page, it probably means you are including irrelevant information or are being unnecessarily verbose. Read the rest of these suggestions and then try to cut your resume down. In the end, though, the content of your resume and how effectively you get it across to a prospective employer or client is what matters; if you need two or three pages to do that, use them.

SAY IT CLEARLY AND CONCISELY

No matter how gorgeous your resume is, it will do you no good if a prospective employer finds it difficult to read. There is only one hard and fast rule of resume writing: Never send out a resume that contains mistakes. Proofread it several times and use your spell-check. For most people, writing a resume is an ongoing process, so remember to check it over every time you make a change. There is absolutely no excuse for sending out a resume with misspelled words or grammatical errors. After you proofread it, ask one or two friends to read it over, too. If you are uncertain about a grammatical construction, change it.

In addition to checking spelling and grammar, you want to make sure that your resume is well written. Resume writing is quite different from other kinds of writing, and it takes some practice. For one thing, most resumes do not use complete sentences. Rather than writing, "As manager of the housewares department, I managed 14 employees and was in charge of ordering $2.5 million worth of merchandise annually," write, "Managed $2.5 million housewares department with 14 employees." All the other rules of grammar apply to writing a resume, however. Tenses and numbers need to match, and double negatives and other awkward constructions are not acceptable. When writing a resume, it is also important to be concise to demonstrate that you are an efficient person.

The ability to communicate well is vital in the mediation field, and it is a skill that a potential employer will value highly. If something on your resume is not easily understood, you will not make a good impression. In addition to effective communication, legal mediators need to demonstrate their talents in organization and analysis. These skills can easily be reflected in your resume.

You demonstrate your communication abilities not only by making sure everything is spelled correctly and is grammatically accurate, but also by how well you write your resume. Word choice contributes to the clarity and persuasiveness of your resume. Experts have long recommended using verbs (action words) rather than nouns to promote yourself in a resume.

MAKE YOUR RESUME COMPUTER FRIENDLY

More and more job applicants are posting their resumes on the Internet, and many large firms are scanning resumes into their computer system,

Job-Search Skills and Interviewing

which allows people to call your resume up on their computers. Once your resume is on the Internet or in a computer system, potential employers will access it by searching for keywords. Keywords are simply words or phrases that indicate areas of expertise within an industry; in this case, the legal profession. Keywords tend to be nouns rather than verbs.

In addition to Internet-posting and in-house scanning, you need a resume that can be successfully sent via e-mail. If you will be applying for jobs online or submitting your resume via e-mail, you will need to create an electronic resume (in addition to a traditional printed resume).

When e-mailing your electronic resume directly to an employer it is wise, as a general rule, to save the document as a rich text (.rtf), or a plain or ASCII text (.txt) file. Contact the employer directly to see which format is preferred.

When you send a resume via e-mail, the message should begin as a cover letter (and contain the same information as a cover letter). You can then either attach the resume file to the e-mail message or paste the resume text within the message, depending on what the employer asks for.

Be sure to include your e-mail address as well as your regular mailing address and phone number(s) within all e-mail correspondence. Never assume an employer will receive your message and simply hit respond, using their e-mail software to contact you. It is always a good idea to put the most important information in the top third of your resume, where it can readily be seen in case the potential employer does not print it out.

GUIDELINES FOR CREATING AN ELECTRONIC RESUME

Set the left and right margins on the document so that 6.5 inches of text will be displayed per line. This will ensure that the text will not automatically wrap to the next line (unless you want it to).

Use a basic, 12-point text font, such as Times New Roman.

Bullets or other symbols may not translate well at the other end. Instead, use asterisks (*) or a dashes (-) which are normal keys. Instead of using the percentage sign (%) spell out the word percent.

Use the spell-check feature of the software you used to create your electronic resume and then proofread the document carefully. Just as applicant-tracking software is designed to pick out keywords from your resume that showcase you as a qualified applicant, these same software packages used by employers can also instantly count the number of typos and spelling errors in your document and report that to an employer as well.

Avoid using multiple columns, tables, or charts within your document.

Within the text, avoid abbreviations—spell everything out. For example, use the word Director, not Dir., or Vice President as opposed to VP. For academic degrees, however, it is acceptable to MBA, BA, PhD, and the like.

Although formatting your electronic resume properly is critical to having it scanned or read correctly, it is what you actually say in your resume that will ultimately get you hired. According to Rebecca Smith, author of *Electronic Resumes & Online Networking* and the companion website (www.eresumes.com),

> Keywords are the basis of the electronic search and retrieval process. They provide the context from which to search for a resume in a database, whether the database is a proprietary one that serves a specific purpose, or whether it is a Web-based search engine that serves the general public. Keywords are a tool to browse quickly without having to access the complete text. Keywords are used to identify and retrieve a resume for the user.
>
> Employers and recruiters generally search resume databases using keywords—nouns and phrases that highlight technical and professional areas of expertise, industry-related jargon, projects, achievements, special task forces, and other distinctive features about a prospect's work history.

The emphasis is not on trying to second-guess every possible keyword a recruiter may use to find your resume. Your focus is on selecting and organizing your resume's content to highlight those keywords for a variety of online situations. The idea is to identify all possible keywords that are appropriate to your skills and accomplishments that support the kind of jobs you are looking for. But to do that, you must apply traditional resume writing principles to the concept of extracting those keywords from your resume. Once you have written your resume, you can identify your strategic keywords based on how you imagine people will search for your resume.

The keywords you incorporate into your resume should support or be relevant to your job objective. Some of the best places within your resume to incorporate keywords are when you are listing

job titles
responsibilities
accomplishments
skills
certifications

Industry-related buzzwords, job-related technical jargon, licenses, and degrees are among the other opportunities you will have to come up with keywords to add to your electronic resume. If you are posting your resume on the Internet, look for the categories that websites use and make sure you use them, too. Be sure the word legal mediator appears somewhere on your resume, and use accepted professional jargon. Do not, for example, write that you are interested in hearing cases involving businesses. Someone scanning your resume will probably look for the words *commercial disputes*.

For scanned resumes, *manager* is a better bet than *managed*. Verbs such as *initiated*, *inspired*, and *directed* probably will not be keywords either. You can still use verbs—just make sure they do not take the place of other possible keywords or you cannot substitute other possible keywords.

Keywords are often connected by *and* rather than by *or*. If an employer is looking for someone interested in being a divorce mediator who can also handle disputes regarding child custody and visitation, your resume will not come up if it contains only divorce mediation and not child custody. It may be helpful to look at some of the resumes posted on the Internet; think about the keywords you would use to search for them. The successful hits you get will indicate the words you should be using.

An excellent resource for helping you select the best keywords to use in your electronic resume is *The Occupational Outlook Handbook* (published by the U.S. Department of Labor). This publication is available, free of charge, online (www.bls.gov/oco/ocos114.htm); a printed edition can also be found at most public libraries.

WHAT GOES ON A RESUME

When you are just starting out, it is tempting to try to put everything you can think of on your resume to try to make it look more substantial. Resist the temptation. Stick to what is important and pertinent. Surrounding the important information with a lot of white space will make it stand out more, and that is good—this is a basic principle of effective advertising.

Under no circumstances should you include personal information such as age, gender, religion, health, marital status, or number of children. For one thing, it is illegal for employers to ask about those things, and it is illegal for a reason: They have nothing to do with how well a person can do a job. The only personal information that belongs on your resume is your contact information: name, address, phone number, cell phone number, and e-mail address, along with a fax number if you have one. By the way, your name and contact information should be on every page you send, in case the pages get separated.

People often overlook or discount volunteer work when composing their resumes. This is a mistake. For one thing, you gain skills and experience from these jobs just as you do from jobs you are paid for. Volunteering also indicates that you work well with others and that you are committed to your community. (Keep this in mind as you go through your mediation training; if you are short on experience, you might think about volunteering.) Also, make sure your resume includes any memberships and activities in professional organizations; they help demonstrate your commitment to the profession.

Another way to make yourself look more experienced is by including your internships. Some new graduates, be they graduates of certificate programs or of degree-bearing ones, overlook this, considering internships to be just part of school. But for most newly graduated mediators, it is their only mediation experience and perhaps their only work experience. The point of internships is to give you on-the-job training. You learned things at internships that will help you on a new job; be sure to include them.

Make sure you do not overlook any previous experience. Applicants who are changing careers sometimes think the things they did in their previous work life do not apply to being a legal mediator, but the contrary is true. Any job you held taught you something that will make you a better mediator. At the very least, it taught you the responsibility of showing up for work regularly and on time. No doubt you also learned about working with others and organizing your time. Beyond that, many jobs provide you with experience that will be highly valued by employers or clients. A career such as medicine, accounting, real estate, human resources, education, business, social work, psychology, and insurance, as well as many others, will be considered a hiring plus by potential employers.

In addition to work experience, you may have life experience that should be emphasized for legal employers. Did you help a spouse in a business? Were you a candidate for public office? Any number of experiences can add to your attractiveness as a legal mediator candidate. Especially if you do not have a great deal of work experience, be creative with other things you have done in your life. *Be creative* does not mean *lie*. Just think about things you have done that have taught you lessons that are valuable for a legal mediator. Find a way to include those experiences on your resume or in your cover letter.

HOW TO TAILOR YOUR RESUME

Each time you send out a resume, whether in response to an ad or following up on a networking lead or even a cold contact, you should concentrate on tailoring your approach for the employer you are contacting. Earlier, it was recommended that you should spend some time pursuing your dream job. It may be that you have more than one dream job, and no doubt you will also be watching out for the close-to-dream-job opening.

Let us say you are interested in being a divorce mediator, particularly in cases involving children and custody battles, because every summer in high school, you tutored at a children's camp for underprivileged children and you really liked helping children. You would probably also be willing to take a position in a large mediation group that does divorces among other things or as mediator for a school or even in a court-based mediation program where you might get to hear a matrimonial case, just to get your foot in the door. Child custody matters are your dream cases; the others are your close-to-dream cases. And if enough time passes, you will be happy to take any mediation position in any kind of office. Right there, you need at least four resumes.

The resume for the family matters and child custody mediation job stresses the work you did with children, the mediation techniques you learned at your internship, and how well you did in the divorce mediation training in school. Although it depends on what format you are using, you may very well stress them in that order. For a mediation position in a large firm that handles family matters, you would probably stress your internship and education—but make sure your divorce experience and your experience with children stand out, too. For the job as a mediator in a school, you would emphasize your experience with children and any of your general academic accomplishments. Finally, for the basic court-based mediation program, you would want your resume to show that you are a generalist and to reflect all your academic achievements.

Most books that tell you how to write a resume include advice about the information you should gather before you start. If you keep all of that information at hand, it will be relatively easy to construct a resume that targets a particular job, concentrating your information so that a prospective employer will see that you are a likely candidate for this opening. In many cases, a few changes to a basic resume are enough to make it appropriate for a particular job opening. One good way to approach tailoring your resume for a particular opening is to take a minute to imagine what you think the job would be like. Based on the description of the job, imagine the major things you would be expected to do from day to day. Then look at your experience and education and decide how to present your information in such a way that the employer will know you are capable of doing those tasks.

Finally, make sure you get your resume to the appropriate person in the appropriate way. If you got the person's name through a networking contact, your contact may deliver it or suggest that you deliver it in person; most likely, though, you should mail it. If you are making a cold contact—that is, if you are contacting a mediation group that you found through your research but that is not actively looking to fill a position—make sure you find out the name of the person in charge of hiring and send your resume to that person. If you are responding to an ad, make sure you do what the ad says. If it directs you to e-mail your resume, e-mail it. If it indicates you should send a writing sample, make sure you include one. (If you are using a sample you wrote on a job or internship, you must black out all names and any other identifying information.) Demonstrate your ability to attend to detail.

OVERALL CONTENT

Use the following questionnaire to gather the information you will need for your resume.

Contact Information

The only personal information that belongs on your resume is your name (on every page, if your resume exceeds one page in length), address, phone number, fax number, and e-mail address.

> Full name:
> Permanent street address:
> City, state, zip:
> Daytime telephone number:
> Evening telephone number:
> Mobile phone number (optional):
> Fax number (optional):
> E-mail address:
> Personal website address/online portfolio URL:
> School address (if applicable):
> Your phone number at school (if applicable):

Job or Career Objectives

Write a short description of the job you are seeking. Be sure to include as much information as possible about how you can use your skills to the employer's benefit. Later, you will condense this answer into one short sentence.
What is the job title you are looking to find (for example, legal mediator)?

Educational Background

Be sure to include your internships in this section. For most recent graduates, it is their only mediation experience and perhaps their only work experience.

Include the skills you learned that will be applicable to the position for which you are applying.

List the most recent college, university, or certificate program you have attended:

City/state:
What year did you start?
Graduation month/year:
Degree(s) and/or award(s) earned:
Your major(s):
Your minor(s):
List some of your most impressive accomplishments, extracurricular activities, club affiliations, and the like:
List computer courses you have taken that help qualify you for the job you are seeking:
Grade point average (GPA):

Other colleges/universities you have attended:
City/state:
What year did you start?
Graduation month/year:
Degree(s) and/or award(s) earned:
Your major(s):
Your minor(s):
List some of your most impressive accomplishments, extracurricular activities, club affiliations, and the like:
List computer courses you have taken that help qualify you for the job you are seeking:
Grade point average (GPA):
High school attended:
City/state:
Graduation date:
Grade point average (GPA):
List the names and phone numbers of one or two current or past professors, teachers, or guidance counselors you can contact about obtaining a letter of recommendation or give as a reference:

Personal Skills and Abilities

Your personal skill set (the combination of skills you possess) is something that differentiates you from everyone else. Skills that are marketable in the workplace are not always taught in school, however. Your ability to manage people, stay cool under pressure, remain organized, surf the Internet, use software applications, speak in public, communicate well in writing, communicate in multiple languages, or perform research are all examples of marketable skills.

When reading job descriptions or help wanted ads, pay careful attention to the wording used to describe what the employer is looking for. As you customize your resume for a specific employer, you will want to match up what the employer is looking for with your own qualifications as closely as possible. Try to utilize the wording provided by the employer within the classified ad or job description.

What do you believe is your most marketable skill? Why?

List three or four specific examples of how you have used this skill in the past while at work. What was accomplished as a result?

1. _____
2. _____
3. _____
4. _____

What keywords or buzzwords can be used to describe your skill?

What is another of your marketable skills?

Provide at least three examples of how you have used this skill in the workplace:

1. _____
2. _____
3. _____

What unusual or unique skill(s) do you possess that help you stand out from other applicants applying for the same types of positions as you?

How have you already proven that this skill is useful in the workplace?

What computer skills do you possess?

What computer software packages are you proficient in (such as Microsoft Office, Word, Excel, PowerPoint, FrontPage, SAGA, InterMediate, or Outlook)?

Thinking carefully, what skills do you believe you currently lack?

What skills do you have that need to be polished or enhanced to make you a more appealing candidate?

What options are available to you either to obtain or to brush up on the skills you believe need improvement (for example, evening or weekend classes at a college or university, adult education classes, seminars, books, home study courses, or on-the-job training)?

In what time frame could you realistically obtain this training?

Work and Employment History

Complete the following employment-related questions for all of your previous employers, including part-time or summer jobs held while in school, as well as temp jobs, internships, and volunteering. You probably will not want to reveal your past earning history to a potential employer, but you may want this information available as reference when you begin negotiating your future salary, benefits, and overall compensation package.

Most recent employer:
City/state:

Job-Search Skills and Interviewing

Year you began work:
Year you stopped working (write *present* if still employed):
Job title:
Job description:
Reason for leaving:

What were your three proudest accomplishments while holding this job?

1. _____

2. _____

3. _____

Contact person at the company who can provide a reference:
Contact person's phone number:
Annual salary earned:

Employer:
City/state:
Year you began work:
Year you stopped working (write *present* if still employed):
Job title:
Job description:
Reason for leaving:

What were your three proudest accomplishments while holding this job?

1. _____

2. _____

3. _____

Contact person at the company who can provide a reference:
Contact person's phone number:
Annual salary earned:

Military Service (If Applicable)

Branch served in:
Years served:
Highest rank achieved:
Decorations or awards earned:
Special skills or training you obtained:

Professional Accreditations and Licenses

List any and all of the professional accreditations and/or licenses you have earned thus far in your career. Be sure to highlight items that directly relate to the job(s) you will be applying for.

Hobbies and Special Interests

List any hobbies or special interests you have that are not necessarily work related, but that potentially could separate you from the competition. Make sure to include any volunteer work you may have done, any internships you have held, or any courses or workshops you have taken. Even if they had little to do with mediation, try to think about how the courses, internships, or volunteer work may help you be a better mediator. Maybe the volunteer work aroused your interest in your community, or maybe you saw many opportunities for mediation at your internship. It is especially important to include these items if you do not have much work experience. Can any of the skills utilized in your hobby be adapted for the workplace?

What nonprofessional clubs or organizations do you belong to or actively participate in?

Personal and Professional Ambitions

You may not want to share these on your resume, but answering the following questions will help you focus your search and prepare for possible interviewing topics.

What are your long-term goals?
Personal:
Professional:
Financial:

For your personal, professional, and financial goals, what are five smaller, short-term goals you can begin working toward achieving right now that will help you ultimately achieve each of your long-term goals?

Short-term personal goals:

1. _____
2. _____
3. _____
4. _____
5. _____

Short-term professional goals:

1. _____
2. _____
3. _____
4. _____
5. _____

Short-term financial goals:

1. _____
2. _____
3. _____

4. _____

5. _____

Will the job(s) you will be applying for help you achieve your long-term goals and objectives? If yes, how? If no, why not?

Describe your current personal, professional, and financial situation.

What would you most like to improve about your life overall?

What are a few things you can do, starting immediately, to bring about positive changes in your personal, professional, or financial life?

Where would you like to be personally, professionally, and financially five and ten years down the road?

What needs to be done to achieve these long-term goals or objectives?

What are some of the qualities about your personality that you are most proud of?

What are some of the qualities about your personality that you believe need improvement?

What do others most like about you?

What do you think others least like about you?

If you decided to pursue additional education, what would you study and why? How would this help you professionally?

If you had more free time, what would you spend it doing?

List several accomplishments in your personal and professional life that you are most proud of. Why did you choose these things?

Job-Search Skills and Interviewing

1. _____
2. _____
3. _____
4. _____
5. _____

What were your strongest and favorite subjects in school? Is there a way to incorporate these interests into the job(s) or career path you are pursuing?

What do you believe is your biggest weakness? Why would an employer not hire you?

What would be the ideal atmosphere for you to work in? Do you prefer a large corporate atmosphere, working at home, or working in a small office?

List five qualities about a new job that would make it the ideal employment opportunity for you:

1. _____
2. _____
3. _____
4. _____
5. _____

What did you like most about the last place you worked?

What did you like least about the last place you worked?

What work-related tasks are you particularly good at?

What type of coworkers would you prefer to have?

When it comes to work-related benefits and perks, what is most important to you?

When you are recognized for doing a good job at work, how do you like to be rewarded?

If you were to write a help-wanted ad describing your dream job, what would the ad say?

COMMON RESUME ERRORS TO AVOID

Stretching the truth. A growing number of employers are verifying all resume information. If you are caught lying, you will not be offered a job, or you could be fired later if it is discovered that you were not truthful.

Including any references to money. This includes mentioning your past salary or how much you are looking to earn in your resume and cover letter.

Including on your resume the reasons that you stopped working for an employer, switched jobs, or are currently looking for a new job. Do not include a line in your resume saying *Unemployed* or *Out of Work* along with the corresponding dates to fill a time gap.

Having a typo or a grammatical error in a resume. If you refuse to take the time necessary to proofread your resume, why should an employer assume you would take the time needed to do your job properly if you were hired?

Using long paragraphs to describe past work experience. Use a bulleted (or asterisked) list instead. Most employers will spend less than one minute initially reading a resume.

Following are two sample resumes. The first is for an applicant who wants to highlight both his previous experience in the field of personal injury and his educational background. The second is for an applicant who has more education than experience.

MARK MEDIATOR

1234 Broadway

Mytown, ST 00000

Phone and fax: 007-555-5678

E-mail: mark89@online.com

OBJECTIVE

To work as a mediator in a position that allows me to utilize and enhance my knowledge and education in conflict resolution as well as to make use of my experience in personal injury.

EXPERIENCE

September–November 2006

Mediation Internship, Community Mediation Services, 180 West Bubba Street, Mytown, ST 00000; 007-555-3456

Duties:

Answered multiline telephones

Greeted the public

Assisted with scheduling mediations

Assisted with case management

Acted as administrative support for the mediators by gathering the facts of the case and booking expert witnesses

Helped draft agreements to mediate

Filed documents

January 2002–April 2006

Paralegal for Plaintiff's Personal Injury Firm, Smith & David, LLC, 1440 Ivy Road, Mytown, ST 00000; 007-555-1040

Duties:

Interviewed clients

Managed the attorney's calendar

Drafted all legal pleadings

Prepared cases for settlement

January 2001–Present

Volunteer, Community Mediation Services, RR 1, Mytown, ST 00000; 007-555-9876

Duties:

Performed clerical duties

Prepared mediation agreements

Sat in on several mediations

EDUCATION

Master of Science, Mediation and Applied Conflict Studies, May 2007

Mediation College, 7890 Troubadour Street, Mytown, ST 00000

Bachelor of Arts, Art History, December 2005

Community College, Eli Hills Campus, Mytown, ST 00000

SKILLS

Fluent in Spanish

JOHN DANIEL
1234 BROADWAY • MYTOWN, ST 00000
PHONE AND FAX: 007-555-5678 • E-MAIL: JOHN89@ONLINE.COM

OBJECTIVE

Entry-level mediation position that allows me to utilize and enhance my mediation training.

EDUCATION

Bachelor of Arts, Certificate in Conflict Resolution & Mediation, May 2006, State University, Mytown, ST 00000

RELEVANT COURSES

Interpersonal Communication

Effective Listening

Conflict Management

The Mediation Process

Internship in Communication

EXPERIENCE

September–December 2006, Mediation Internship, Community Mediation Services, 180 West Bubba Street, Mytown, ST 00000; 007-555-3456

Duties:

Answered multiline telephones

Greeted the public

Assisted with scheduling mediations

Assisted with case management

Acted as administrative support for the mediators by gathering the facts of the case and booking expert witnesses

Helped draft agreements to mediate

Filed documents

September 2004–August 2005, Sales Associate, The Store, 345 Route 66, Mytown, ST 00000; 007-555-6543

Duties:
- Operated cash register
- Stocked shelves
- Assisted customers

January 1993–Present, Volunteer, Dogs and Cats Shelter, RR 1, Mytown, ST 00000; 007-555-9876

Duties:
- Interview adopters
- Write column for newsletter
- Bathe dogs

SKILLS
Fluent in Spanish

ADDENDUM

If you already possess a lot of experience, you may need to attach an addendum to your resume in order to keep it to a reasonable length. Keep your resume to one to two pages, and use an addendum to supply more information for an employer whose attention you have caught. The resume should include all of the most pertinent information, such as work experience and duties at each job, education, academic accomplishments, and special skills. The addendum should include any additional information such as any professional associations to which you belong, extra certifications you hold, community work or volunteering, as well as any boards you sit on.

WRITING A COVER LETTER

Never send out a resume without a cover letter. The cover letter aims your resume directly at the available job; your resume describes in detail why you are the person for the job. If your cover letter is a failure, your resume will get only a cursory glance at best. Your cover letter should demonstrate that you are a good candidate for the job.

Most people consider writing cover letters to be a painful chore. In fact, though, they are another opportunity to demonstrate your writing skills as well as your ability to organize and analyze. Although you tailor your resume to some degree for different job openings, employers expect that you will send the same resume to several potential employers. The cover letter, on the other hand, should be personalized and directed to the particular job opening.

HOW TO FORMAT YOUR COVER LETTER

Your cover letter needs to grab the attention of the reader—but not because it is so bizarre that it will be posted on the office bulletin board for everyone to laugh at. As with your resume, avoid fancy fonts and stationery; instead, choose something that matches or coordinates with your resume. Your cover letter should always be printed on good paper. Consider using letterhead printed with your name, address, phone and fax numbers, and e-mail address. You need not spend a lot of money to have letterhead stationery printed; you can create it on your computer.

A cover letter should be composed like a business letter. It should include your address (preferably in the letterhead), the date, the name and address of the person the letter is sent to, and a salutation. At the end of the body of the letter, you should include a closing (such as *Sincerely* or *Respectfully*), and your signature, with your name typed out below it. Other formatting choices are up to you—for example, whether you prefer block paragraphs or indented paragraphs and whether you write *enc.* at the very bottom, indicating there is material (your resume) enclosed with the letter.

Rarely do you need a cover letter that is more than one page. On occasion, an advertisement for a job will ask for a resume and a detailed statement of interest (or words to that effect). Sometimes, ads will even ask you to address specific questions or issues in your letter, such as your goals or what you can contribute to the organization. In such cases, you may need to write a letter that is more than one page. Normally, however, your letter should fit on one page.

WRITE CLEARLY AND CONCISELY

Never send out a cover letter with a grammatical or spelling error. Even when you are pressed for time and rushing to get a letter out, make sure to spell-check it and proofread it carefully. If writing letters does not come naturally to you—and writing cover letters does not come naturally to most of us—have someone else read it over as well. It should be accurate,clear, and concise. It serves as a letter of introduction, an extension of your advertisement; it is the first face you show a potential employer.

Your cover letter needs to convince a prospective employer that you are one of the people who should be interviewed for this position. It should begin with some sort of introduction, continue with an explanation of why you are right for this job, and end with a concluding paragraph. As with your resume, it is vital that your cover letter be well written; however, it requires a different writing style. For example, sentence fragments do not belong in a cover letter. In addition, a resume offers a somewhat formal presentation of your background, whereas a cover letter should let a bit of your personality come through. Do not use contractions or slang in a cover letter—but you should view it as your first chance to communicate with a prospective employer. The resume tells employers what you know and what you can do; the cover letter should tell them a little bit about who you are.

WHAT TO INCLUDE IN YOUR COVER LETTER

Much more than a resume, a cover letter is targeted to a particular job. The concentration on a particular job opening is the major component of a cover letter. A cover letter should never read like a form letter; the best way to avoid that is by writing a new letter for every job you apply for. A cover letter does not just repeat the information in your resume but tells the prospective employer why you are the right person for a particular job.

In the first paragraph, you should indicate why you are writing this letter at this time. You might write something along these lines:

"I would like to apply for the mediator position advertised in the April 11 *Sunday Post*."

"I am writing in response to your ad in the February 1 *Sunday Times*."

"I am interested in obtaining a mediator position with your mediation conglomerate."

"If you are looking for a mediator with family matters experience and top-notch conflict resolution training, you will be interested in talking to me."

"We met last July at the American Bar Association dinner. I will be graduating from my mediation program in May."

The first paragraph also usually indicates that your resume is enclosed for consideration, although this may also be in the closing paragraph.

In the body of the cover letter, you want to explain why your training and experience make you the right person for the job. The cover letter provides you with the opportunity to include something that is not on your resume. For example, life experience can be difficult to incorporate into a resume, but is much easier to talk about in a letter. Also, the body of the letter should highlight and summarize the information in your resume. The employer will most likely read your resume, so do not simply repeat the information it contains. So, instead of writing "Before my mediation program, I worked at The Store for two years, and before that at The Shop for three years" try something like, "I have five years of retail experience in which I interacted with the public on a daily basis." The body of the letter is your opportunity to explain why the employer should care about your experience and training.

In the body of the letter, you can also include information about how soon you are available for employment or why (if it is the case) you are applying for a job out of town. You may also include the specifics that you are looking for in a job—especially if they are either nonnegotiable or flattering to the employer. You should definitely make some direct reference to the specific position and organization. Here are some examples:

"I will graduate on May 16 and will be available for employment immediately. A position with your group appeals to me because I understand you do a great deal of medical malpractice work, which is a field I am very interested in. Medical malpractice was one of the electives I chose as a student. In addition, at this time I am looking for part-time employment, and I believe you currently have a part-time opening."

"Although my internship was at the Westchester Supreme Court, I have come to realize that while that work was intensely interesting, I would prefer a position in the private sector that will afford me the opportunity to call on my personal injury experience and my conflict resolution training. I believe your firm is the place for me, and I am certain I would be an asset to you."

"As you look at my resume, you will notice that although I am just now finishing my mediation training, I offer a background in administration and problem solving. Because your company has recently undergone a major expansion, I believe you would find me a valuable addition to your staff."

Finally, the last paragraph (some people prefer it to be two short paragraphs) should thank the person, make a reference to future contact, and offer to provide further information.

"Thank you for your consideration. Please contact me at the address or phone number above if you need any further information."

"I look forward to meeting you to discuss this job opening."

"Thank you, and I look forward to speaking with you in person."

"I would welcome the opportunity to discuss the match between my skills and your needs in more detail. You can contact me at the address or phone number above, except for the week of the 27th, when I will be out of town. Thank you for your time."

A cover letter provides the opportunity for you to sell yourself for a particular job, and it should be tailored that way. The letter should indicate some knowledge about what makes this job better than all the other jobs and what makes you a better candidate than all the other candidates.

SURVIVING YOUR INTERVIEW

When job hunting, you will send out carefully worded resumes and cover letters. Some of the time, you will either get a polite brush-off or no response at all. Waiting for an interview can be quite frustrating. At the same time, the prospect of an interview is daunting to many people: When they finally get one, they would rather do almost anything else—go to the dentist, give the cat a bath, or clean the oven! The tips on the next few pages will not necessarily make your next interview 100% painless, but they will help you can get through it and come out a winner.

Preparing for Your Interview

Mediators are trained to be impartial and treat each party equally. Generally, in mediation, we think this unbiased equality is a good thing, albeit hard to achieve. Preparing for your interview adequately will take you a long way toward feeling on an equal footing with the interviewer. As with writing resumes and cover letters, there are many fine sources of information about job interviews; this book goes over some things that are specific to mediation job hunting, especially when you are after your first job in the field.

Most interviewers will ask, *Why do you want to work here?* Sometimes, the true answer to that question is, *I do not necessarily want to work here; I'd be just as happy down the street, but you have got the opening.* (This is not a good answer!) For every interview, you should be prepared to answer to this question.

If you managed to get an interview without researching the mediation group ahead of time, do so now. (If you researched the group *before* you applied, as you should have, make sure you saved all the information so you can use it now.) Keep researching until you find something that makes you excited about working there. That can sometimes be difficult, but there will always be something. Keep an eye on the newspapers; if you read about an interesting local case and they mention that it was mediated, find out where that mediator works; someday, this may provide you with a reason you want to work at this mediation group.

Even if you are not asked why you want to work at a mediation company, find an opportunity to let your interviewer know you have done your research. Is it a fairly new company or has it been around forever? Is it the largest or one of the smallest groups in town? Did it just settle (or fail to settle) a big case?

In advance of your interview, check the exact address and find out how to get there and where to park. Try on your interview outfit and make sure it is comfortable for both walking and sitting. The night before the interview, make sure you will have prepared everything you need by reviewing the following.

Bring several copies of your resume and a list of references as well as copies of your transcripts. You might consider carrying these documents in a briefcase. (Remember, it is called a briefcase because it is used for carrying briefs. It is a conventional legal tool; use it until you know how formal the mediation group is.) You should also bring with you a good pen and a legal pad in case you want to take notes.

Women should bring a spair pair of pantyhose. Men may want to bring an extra tie in case the situation calls for a more conservative one.

Answering Tough Questions

There are two important things to keep in mind while job hunting. One is that even if you apply and interview for a job, you are not obliged to accept it; the other is that good interviewers will be trying to sell you on coming to work for them.

Understanding that you are not required to take a job just because it is offered makes the interview seem less like a life-or-death situation and more like an opportunity to get to know at least one person at this firm. There are other jobs out there, and although job hunting is not much fun, you will find a job. Realizing that interviewers should be trying to sell you on coming to work for them is helpful, too. Although conducting job interviews is a skill that some people never master, good interviewers want to find a good person to fill the job opening. They already think you are a possibility; even though they may end up hiring someone else, during the interview they should be trying to convince you that you would be very happy working there.

Neither of these points takes away from the fact that you have to sell yourself. But in preparing for the interview, keep in mind that you have certain requirements of your own and that you are meeting these potential employers to find out whether the two of you are a match.

Greet your interviewer with a firm handshake and an enthusiastic smile. Speak with confidence throughout your interview and let your answers convey your assumption that you will be offered the job. For example, phrase your questions this way: *What would my typical day consist of? How many mediators work here, and what are their areas of expertise?* Answer questions in complete sentences but do not ramble on too long in answering any one question. Many hiring managers will ask questions that do not have a right or wrong answer; such questions are intended to evaluate your problem-solving skills.

The world will not end if you stumble over your words or do not know how to answer a particular question or even if you forget your own phone number, but that does not mean you should not prepare for an interview. At a minimum, look over your resume and think about what an interviewer would want to know about you. For example, you might be asked why you want to be a mediator. You will probably be asked which types of cases you like best and least, and why. If you are changing careers, you may be asked why you are changing and what you liked and did not like about your former career. Spend some time thinking about and practicing ways to answer these questions.

As you look at your resume, note any unusual aspects that might elicit questions. For example, I once worked as a cab driver; as long as that was on my resume, I always got asked about it. I was relieved when this experience was more than ten years old and I could leave it off and start talking about other things. If you have a gap in your work history, be prepared to explain why. Also be prepared to talk about the kinds of legal computer software you are familiar with, as well as the kinds of work you have done in an internship or a previous job.

If you are not fresh out of a mediation program but are leaving one position for another, you will no doubt be asked why you are leaving and what your billable hours were. You may be expected to discuss what went well or poorly at that job, how you handled difficult clients or attorneys and what you hope will be different about your new job.

The toughest of the tough questions that you will have to deal with are the illegal ones—and, yes, mediators or those in charge of hiring mediators sometimes ask them. A potential employer is not allowed to ask you about your marital status, whether you have or plan to have children, your age, your religion, or your race (although such questions may be asked on anonymous affirmative action forms). Nor may an interviewer use roundabout techniques to find out (such as *I bet your husband and kids are really proud of you!*). If someone does ask you such a question, you can simply say, *It is illegal for you to ask me that*, and then sit silently until the interviewer says something. Or try to get a handle on why they are asking, and address that. For example, the answer to *Do you have children?* could be *If you are asking if I can travel and work overtime, that is generally not a problem*. Or you can say something like, *I do not understand the question; what is it you want to know?*

Remember that illegal questions are not always obvious. Most interviewers know enough not to say ask your age outright. But they might say, *Will it bother you if your supervisor is younger than you?* If you encounter this kind of situation, think long and hard before you accept a position with this mediation company. Also, if you were referred to this interview through an employment agency or your school's placement office, notify that source that you believe you were asked illegal questions.

Here are some general guidelines to follow when answering questions in an interview.

- ▶ Use complete sentences and proper English.
- ▶ Do not be evasive, especially if asked about negative aspects of your employment history.
- ▶ Never imply that a question is stupid.
- ▶ Do not lie or stretch the truth.
- ▶ Be prepared to answer the same questions several times over. Make sure your answers are consistent, and never reply, *You already asked me that*.
- ▶ Never apologize for negative information regarding your past.
- ▶ Avoid talking down to an interviewer or making them feel less intelligent than you are.

Asking Questions

When we think about the kinds of questions an interviewee should ask in an interview, we often concentrate on what kinds of questions we think we are expected to ask. But the main goal is to ask the things you really want to know. One exception is that you should probably save questions about salary and benefits for a second interview; a first interview is an opportunity to learn more about the firm.

Beyond that, ask about almost anything. You may want to know about the kinds of cases you can expect, whether you will be able to follow cases from start to finish, whether you will have the opportunity to specialize, who manages mediators and determines what cases they hear. These are all legitimate questions. You may also have questions about the resources of the mediation group, such as the computers and library. The number of billable hours you will be expected to produce is certainly something you will want to know.

If the mediation group is large, you can ask about its structure. For example, are the mediators employees or independent contractors? Do mediators have marketing and administrative support? Is there a mediation training program in place? If the group is small, you may ask how many mediators work for the group, whether it plans to hire more in the future, and whether mediators are expected to do significant clerical work. In any size mediation company, you can ask about chances for promotion.

You can ask what a typical day for a mediator at the mediation group is like. Imagine you have been offered this job and another. Think about what you would like to know about this job that would help you decide which one to take.

By the way, you do not need to wait to be asked whether you have any questions. It is perfectly appropriate to ask questions whenever they fit into the interview. For example, if the interviewer tells you that each mediator has a computer, that would be a good time to ask what software they use and whether the firm subscribes to an online service.

The following are common interview questions, along with suggestions on how you can best answer them:

- ▶ What can you tell me about yourself? (Stress your skills and accomplishments. Avoid talking about your family, hobbies, or topics not relevant to your ability to do the job.)
- ▶ Why have you chosen to pursue a career as a mediator? (Give specific reasons and examples.)
- ▶ In your personal or professional life, what has been your greatest failure? (Be open and honest. Everyone has had some type of failure.)

- What did you learn from that experience? (Focus on what you learned from the experience and how it helped you grow as a person.)
- Why did you leave your previous job? (Try to put a positive spin on your answer, especially if you were fired for negative reasons. Company downsizing, a company going out of business, or some other reason that was out of your control is a perfectly acceptable answer. Remember, your answer will probably be verified.)
- What would you consider your biggest accomplishments at your last job? (Talk about what made you a productive employee and a valuable asset to your previous employer. Stress that teamwork was involved in achieving your success and that you work well with others.)
- What are your long-term goals? (Talk about the career path you have been following and where you think this preplanned path will take you in the future. Describe how you believe the job you are applying for is a logical step forward.)
- Why do you think you are the most qualified person to fill this job? (Focus on the positive things that set you apart from the competition: what is unique about you, your skill set, and your past experiences. What work-related experiences do you have that pertain directly to this job?)
- What have you heard about this company that interests you? (Focus on the company's reputation. Refer to positive publicity, personal recommendations from employees, or published information that caught your attention. This shows you have done your research.)
- What can you tell about yourself that isn't listed in your resume? (This is yet another opportunity for you to sell yourself to the employer. Take advantage of the opportunity.)

Avoiding Common Interview Mistakes

Once a potential employer invites you to come in for an interview, do everything within your power to prepare, and avoid the common mistakes often made by applicants. Remember that for every job you apply for, there are probably dozens of other mediators who would like to land that same position.

Job-Search Skills and Interviewing

The following are some of the most common mistakes applicants make while preparing for or participating in job interviews, with tips on how to avoid making these mistakes.

- ▶ Do not skip steps in your interview preparation. Just because you have been invited for an interview, you should not expect to play it by ear. Prior to the interview, spend time doing research about the company, its products or services, and the people you will be meeting with. Use your research to compile a list of intelligent questions to ask the employer. These questions can be about the company, its products or services, its methods of doing business, the responsibilities of the job you are applying for, and so on.
- ▶ Never arrive late for an interview. Arriving even five minutes late for a job interview is equivalent to telling an employer you do not want the job. On the day of the interview, plan on arriving at least ten minutes early, and use the restroom before you begin the actual interview.
- ▶ Do not neglect your appearance. First impressions are crucial. Make sure your clothing is wrinkle-free and clean, that your hair is well groomed, and that your makeup (if applicable) looks professional. Always dress up for an interview, even if the dress code at the company is casual. Also, be sure to brush your teeth prior to an interview, especially if you have recently eaten.
- ▶ Avoid drinking any beverages containing caffeine before an interview. Chances are, you are already nervous; drinking coffee or soda will not calm you down.
- ▶ When it is time for you to answer questions, always use complete sentences.
- ▶ Never bring up salary, benefits, or vacation time during the initial interview. Instead, focus on how you (with all of your skills, experience, and education) can become a valuable asset to the company. Allow the employer to bring up the compensation package to be offered.
- ▶ Refrain from discussing your past earning history or what you are hoping to earn. An employer typically looks for the best possible employees for the lowest possible price. Let the employer make you an offer first. When asked, tell the interviewer you are looking for a salary and benefits package in line with what is standard in the industry

for someone with your qualifications and experience. Try to avoid stating an actual dollar figure.
- ▶ During the interview, avoid personal topics. As mentioned earlier, there are questions that an employer may not legally ask during an interview or on an employment application. In addition to these topics, refrain from discussing sex, religion, politics, and any other personal or potentially controversial topics.
- ▶ Never insult the interviewer. What you might perceive as a stupid or irrelevant question may simply be the interviewer's way of seeing how you respond. Some questions are asked to test your morals or determine your level of honesty. Other types of questions are used simply to see how you would react in a tough situation. Try to avoid getting caught up in trick questions. Never tell an interviewer that a question is stupid or irrelevant.
- ▶ Throughout the interview, keep your body language under control. For example, if you habitually tap your foot when nervous, make sure you are aware of this habit so you can control it in an interview situation.
- ▶ If your job interview takes place over lunch or dinner, refrain from drinking alcohol of any kind.

FOLLOWING UP ON YOUR INTERVIEW

You should follow up every interview with a letter. There is some disagreement about the form this letter should take. One opinion is that a handwritten thank you note to everyone you meet in an interview is appropriate. On the other hand, a printed letter on letterhead looks more professional. If your handwriting is not particularly legible, you should definitely type your thank you letters. Other than that, check with your placement office and fellow mediation job hunters to determine the tradition in your area. You should do what is commonly accepted in your area and what makes you feel most comfortable. Note that there may be times when you have no choice but to handwrite a letter (if you are out of town or at a professional conference, for example).

Whether handwritten or typed, your letter should include a warm thank you for the interviewer's time and should reiterate your enthusiasm for the job. You should also say something that is specific to your interview to give it a personal touch. Thank you letters are generally quite short. Here are a few examples.

- "I enjoyed meeting with you yesterday to discuss the mediation position at JAMS, the Resolution Experts. In addition to providing a good deal of information, you made me very enthusiastic about the position. I was pleased to have the opportunity to meet Mr. Smith; I can see that he will be difficult to replace. I am gratified to be considered for the position."
- "Thank you so much for the time you spent with me yesterday. I really appreciated the tour of the office and the information you shared about the mediation position. By the way, I double-checked when I got home, and the case I was trying to think of was *Marbury v. Madison*."
- "The mediation position we discussed yesterday certainly sounds like a challenging one. After reviewing the information you gave me about your needs for this job, I am convinced that I am the right person for the position. Thank you for the time and consideration you gave me. I look forward to hearing from you again soon."

Basically, a follow-up letter reminds employers who you are and makes you stand out from the crowd, clarifies (but only if necessary) anything that you were unable to make clear in the interview, and lets employers know that you really want this job.

As you begin your job hunt, keep in mind that you are not looking for just any job but for a good job, one you will enjoy and feel challenged by. At each stage of the hunt—researching the market, sending out resumes and cover letters, having interviews, and accepting or rejecting offers—keep in mind the principles of job hunting. You need to decide whom you are going to contact, you have to advertise yourself, and you have to sell yourself. Remember that each of these involves particular activities and particular ways of thinking about yourself and what you want, as well as marketing yourself to appeal to employers. Once you have finished an internship or mediation program and gotten some experience, you have a lot to offer to any employer. Keep this in mind throughout the process: You are not begging for a job; you are trying to find an employer who will be a match for your skills and talents.

Becoming a LEGAL MEDIATOR

THE INSIDE TRACK

What are your feelings on there being no formal educational requirements to become a mediator?

Shelly Rossoff Olsen, Esq.:

I think being a really good mediator is intuitive, an instinct you have—maybe from being a part of a dysfunctional family or just being human. I haven't had any official mediation training and I don't think it's necessary; in fact, I think it can be a bit of a waste of time. The skills you need to be a really good mediator are talents you just have or not.

Hon. John P. DiBlasi (Retired):

You have to get training. The process is a very specific one. I have 60-70 CLE credits in mediation and I continue to push myself to get more, to keep reading, to learn about new techniques. I have been a trial attorney and judge for fifteen years and I constantly look to continue my training.

Hon. Elizabeth Bonina:

I haven't had any formal mediation training but I sat on the bench for twelve years! As a judge we are trained to be professionally neutral. I've taken that skill with me into mediating. However, I do not see how requiring training for mediators would hurt.

CHAPTER eight

HOW TO SUCCEED ONCE YOU HAVE LANDED THE JOB

The key to success in any new endeavor is understanding what the people around you expect of you, what you can expect of them, and how those expectations can be made to work together so that you will not only succeed but be comfortable and maybe even enjoy yourself as well. In this chapter, you will find tips on fitting into the ADR work environment as well as resources from which you can get general information about fitting into your working environment and dealing with difficult people.

If I were to summarize in one sentence the single most important principle I have learned in the field of interpersonal relations, it would be this: Seek first to understand, then to be understood. This principle is the key to effective interpersonal communication.
  —Stephen Covey (1932–)

BEING A mediator is not for everyone. But for those who make the decision to enter legal mediation, it is also extremely fulfilling: You facilitate the resolution of conflicts in a way that lets people feel in control of their own lives. Your success as part of an organization or in an independent practice, however, depends on many factors.

JOINING A GROUP OR GOING IT ALONE

If you possess an entrepreneurial spirit, a love of business, and a desire to be your own boss, you may decide to be a solo practitioner. If you would prefer to focus solely on hearing cases and do not relish administrative, advertising, and staffing duties, you may decide to join a mediation group. Both are viable options for a mediator, though each has its pros and cons.

FITTING INTO THE WORKPLACE CULTURE

Whether you join a mediation group or decide to practice on your own, you will have to make sure you fit into the culture. If you work for yourself, you do not want to discourage potential clients by not looking the part. Of course, if the practice is yours, you may choose to be a unique and eccentric mediator who does not follow the established cultural norms, but that can be risky, especially if you are not yet established. If you decide to join a mediation group, you will be obliged to follow the existing culture.

Typically, the mediation workplace culture looks a lot like the law firm culture because as a mediator you work closely with various legal professionals who expect a certain standard. However, mediation is a new and emerging field that is not yet part of the mainstream, so it has a degree of flexibility and certainly a lesser degree of formality. For example, a mediation conglomerate today could not require all mediators to wear ties because so many mediators now are women. Still, in most mediation groups men and women alike dress conservatively. Until you find out otherwise, you should dress and behave on your new job as if you are working in an old established profession. This may seem counterintuitive considering the new and alternative nature of mediation, but remember that mediation as an industry is closely tied to the legal field.

Of course, if you go to work for the community mediator crowd, you will find a much less conservative, much more casual work culture. In offices like these, jeans and T-shirts may be appropriate attire. Somewhere between them and the old, established large groups are the small groups and solo practitioners, where style is determined much more by the individuals than by anything else. The safest thing is to take your cue from those around you. You may not meet any other mediators in the interview and hiring process, but if you do, dress according to their style for your first couple of days. If in doubt at first, wear businesslike attire.

Once you have worked in a place for a while, you will know what is acceptable. Fitting into the workplace culture is about a lot more than what you wear, however. Some mediation groups have established traditions, and it will be to your benefit to figure them out. There may be unspoken rules about how to do your marketing, for example, do you market yourself as a mediator or do you market the group? In some larger mediation groups where many high profile cases are heard, you may be expected to be extra formal in your attire and your language.

There are two ways to ensure that you will fit into your workplace culture. Realize that there *is* a culture and that you may not know what it is. Then keep your eyes open and act the way other people act. If no one brings a sack lunch and eats it in the conference room, do not immediately take it upon yourself to start a new trend. The other way to learn the ropes is to get yourself a mentor as soon as possible (see the section on Finding a Mentor later in this chapter).

MANAGING WORK RELATIONSHIPS

Basic Rules

When it comes to building and maintaining professional relationships, some basic rules apply to any workplace. In mediation, you work primarily on your own. You mediate the cases on your own and are bound by confidentiality rules, so you are not allowed to discuss the details of the case. However, in a mediation group you will be surrounded by other mediators, and you want to make sure you have a good relationship with them.

Sometimes Peace Is Better Than Justice

You may be absolutely, 100% sure you are right about a specific situation. Unfortunately, you may have coworkers who doubt you or who flatly disagree with you. This is a common occurrence in the workplace.

In some situations, you need to assert your position and convince the disbelievers to trust your judgment. Your previous track record and reputation will go a long way in helping convince people to trust your opinions, ideas, and decisions. However, you should carefully consider the gravity of any situation before you assert yourself, choosing your battles wisely. For instance, go ahead and argue your position if you can prevent a catastrophe, but in matters of taste, opinion, or preference, you may want to leave the situation alone or accept the decisions of your superiors. Let your recommendation(s) be known, but do not argue your point relentlessly. Sometimes people will not listen to you even when you are right. Always be open to compromise and be willing to listen to and consider the options and ideas of others.

Never Burn Your Bridges
If you are in a disagreement, if you are leaving one employment situation for another, or if a project is ending, always leave the work relationship on a good note. Keep in mind that your professional reputation will follow you throughout your career. It takes years to build a positive reputation but a single mistake can destroy it.

When changing jobs, do not take the opportunity to vent negative thoughts and feelings before you leave. Although it might make you feel good in the short term, it will have a detrimental, lasting effect on your career and on people's perception of you. Someone you insulted could become your boss some day or be in a position to help you down the line. The mediation industry is a close-knit community, and many people know one another, either in person or by reputation.

If you wind up acting unprofessionally toward someone, even if you never interact with that person again, he or she will have contact with many other people and may describe you as hard to work with or rude. Your work reputation is very important; do not tarnish it by burning your bridges.

When changing employment situations, do so in a professional manner. There are countless reasons why someone leaves one job to pursue a career with another, but to maintain a good reputation within the industry, it is important to act professionally when you actually quit. Even if you think your boss is incompetent, never let your negative feelings cause you to act unprofessionally in the heat of anger.

Instead, if you get into a major disagreement with your employer, do not make an impulsive decision to quit. Spend a few days thinking it over. If you end up deciding it is time to move on, start looking for a new job before actually tendering your resignation with your current employer. As a general

How to Succeed Once You Have Landed the Job

rule, even if you are not getting along with your boss or coworkers, it is never a good idea to quit your current job until you have lined up a new one.

Once you have actually landed that new job, be prepared to give your current employer the traditional two weeks' notice. Arrange a private meeting with your boss or other appropriate person within the company, and offer your resignation in person. Following up your verbal resignation in writing with a friendly and professional letter. Some people give notice and then use their accumulated vacation or sick days to avoid showing up for work. This is not appropriate behavior. Even a new employer who wants you to start work immediately will almost always understand that, as a matter of loyalty and professional courtesy, you need to stay with your current employer for two weeks after giving your notice.

During those last two weeks on the job, offer to do whatever you can to maintain a positive relationship with your coworkers and boss, such as offering to train your replacement. Make your exit from the mediation group as smooth as possible. Purposely causing problems, stealing from the employer, or sabotaging business deals are all unethical and totally inappropriate actions. Some groups will request your immediate departure when you quit, and will cut off your computer access and escort you out of the building, especially if you are leaving on a negative note. Prior to quitting, try to determine how past coworkers were treated, so you will know what to expect.

As you actually leave the company for the last time, take with you only your personal belongings and nothing that is considered the company's property. Make a point to return directly to your boss your office keys and any company-owned equipment in your possession. If possible, for your protection, obtain a written memo stating that everything was returned promptly and in working order.

Keep Your Work and Social Life Separate

You were hired to do a job, not to make new friends and meet potential dates. Although it is important to be friendly and to form positive relationships with the people you work with, you should understand the risks associated with becoming too close. Personal relationships can interfere with your job performance, and your job performance can weaken or destroy a relationship. Consider that you might be asked to rate a coworker's job performance, and the coworker happens to be your best friend. Unless your friend is perfect in every way, you will have to compromise either the rating you were asked to give or your friendship. You may also find yourself in the position of having to take work direction from a buddy, or fire someone with whom you have become good friends. Such situations can present major challenges.

The challenges associated with at-work romances can even lead to disaster. Imagine these situations again, substituting a romantic partner for the friend. What was difficult then seems nearly impossible in this case. Not only are you endangering your job performance and the relationship, but you may also be setting yourself up to lose your job. Many companies and corporations frown upon office romances, and some firms have strict policies against them. Depending upon where you work, you could end up looking for another job if your coworkers find out about your romance.

Sexual Harassment

The legal definition of sexual harassment is generally based on the way the recipient feels about the behavior. If the behavior makes someone uncomfortable, it is probably inappropriate and should be reported. Most companies have a policy about sexual harassment in place, and that policy should include the way an employee is expected to report it. And remember: Men can be the victims of sexual harassment and women can be the perpetrators.

The Coworker Relationship

In any work situation you are apt to run into difficult coworkers. Books are available that give advice about dealing with coworkers who backstab, undercut, or short-circuit you. In general, the best advice is to learn about the personnel structure of the firm you are working in. Most likely there is a manager or someone in charge of human resources with whom you can consult if problems with your coworkers reach a level of seriousness that warrants it.

How to Succeed Once You Have Landed the Job

The Client Relationship

In a great many mediation jobs, more of your time will be spent with clients than with coworkers. Typically, people come to see a mediator because they are facing a dispute that they would like to have resolved. Perhaps they are getting divorced or have been injured in a car accident or are having trouble getting along with their landlord. They need help negotiating a settlement. None of these situations are pleasant. Clients are often in distress and want you to wave a magic wand to make all the bad go away. Unfortunately, that is not how things work.

Remember that the goal of the whole process is that the clients leave the mediation feeling better than before. This can be quite a challenge because when you interview a client, your questions are forcing thoughts to the surface that most people would rather keep tucked away. Imagine how you yourself would feel if someone asked you questions like these:

- ▶ Tell me about all your debts and assets.
- ▶ Are you afraid your ex-spouse will harm your child?
- ▶ Tell me, in detail, what you remember from the accident?

You need excellent counseling and communication skills to handle such situations. In addition to reading books and getting lots of training, observe the people you work with who seem to be good at counseling and follow their example. Always keep in mind that although clients probably wish they did not have to be seeing you, it is nothing personal.

Your clients probably know very little about what exactly mediators are and what they do. Therefore, they may either be reluctant to talk to you, seeing you as a kind of makeshift judge, or they may pressure you for legal opinions. In the first instance, a professional demeanor on your part will go a long way toward gaining a reluctant client's confidence. You might remind clients about the time and money they are saving by going this route and that you are here to help facilitate the resolution of their case. In the second instance, remember that engaging in the unauthorized practice of law could jeopardize your job and even your career. Do not do it; explain, kindly, that it is not your place to give legal advice and that the client should ask the attorney, or offer to pass the question along. This does not mean you can never answer a question; of course you will and should exercise your independent judgment. But do not let a weeping client talk you into suggesting—just this once—which bankruptcy chapter to file.

Managing Your Time

Effective time management is crucial to a mediation practice. A great deal of your schedule is determined by someone else. You may be immersed in a long drawn-out mediation and know that you have several more waiting for you.

As a mediator, you may be responsible for keeping your own schedule. A variety of computer programs are available to help you do this. Never, ever think you will remember something without writing it down. In large mediation groups, there may be one person whose job is doing the entire calendar. However it is handled, the information has to get to the right place; a computer program does not know you have a mediation next week unless you tell it so. Make sure you come up with some surefire method for doing your part of the calendaring and that you build in plenty of time to prepare for the session.

Budgeting Time for Projects

Remember that most of a mediator's schedule is determined by someone else. Then remember that you will probably be working for several clients. Now picture several clients handing you cases that take three days to prepare but they all want them heard tomorrow.

Relax. Just because somebody says they want something done tomorrow does not necessarily mean it must actually happen tomorrow. Often it just makes people feel important to say, *This case is top priority*. Also, no matter how much you want to please your bosses, you cannot possibly take on more than one three-day case and have them all done tomorrow (whether you could do even just one is doubtful). Most bosses are reasonable people who know that. You will not be fired for saying *I cannot do that* to a second and even a third request. Finally, just because someone asked *you* first does not mean that person's task is more urgent. The key to working out such priorities is to get everybody together (insofar as possible) and figure out which case really *must* be heard tomorrow and which can wait or be done by someone else. You will save time if you get this kind of information at the outset rather than waiting until you are swamped.

The main points of organization are communication and knowledge. Find out as much as you can about each case, and keep your bosses informed about your progress. For your own sanity, bear in mind that people who like crises seem to be drawn to the law. Some people believe—rightly or wrongly—that they are more productive when they work in crisis mode. If you are one of those types, you will fit right in; if not, you will quickly become valued as the rock—the calm, organized person everyone else can count on.

FINDING A MENTOR

A mentor is a person who is almost as dedicated to advancing your career as you are. In addition, a mentor needs to have the knowledge and experience to help you advance. The typical mentor is a seasoned and established mediator in your mediation group. But a mentor also can be a professor or a teacher or someone you met through a professional organization.

Mentors can be invaluable in helping you succeed in your career—and that means *succeed* in the broadest sense, not just as in getting a promotion. A good mentor not only advises and helps you advance in your career, but also is interested in helping you fit in at your job and listening when you need to talk out a problem. A mentor is a combination of friend and teacher.

You are probably thinking, *Sounds good; how do I find one of those?* That, of course, is the difficult part. Aggressively seeking out a mentor may lead to a very insincere—and, therefore, uncomfortable—relationship. Instead, just keep the idea of a mentor in the back of your mind. If the mediator in the next office, who has worked at the company for several years, asks you to lunch, go. Then ask a lot of questions. Ask what is best and worst about working there, ask about interesting cases from the past; in other words, demonstrate that you are interested and that you believe this person has a lot of answers. No matter how well you seem to hit it off the first time, try a few more times. Next time, ask the other mediator out to lunch yourself. If you are on the same wavelength, you may have found yourself a mentor. If not, you have gained a lot of useful information about the company, maybe even including some ideas about other people you could explore as a possible mentor.

Becoming a Mentor

You should also strive to be a mentor yourself. When you are fresh out of a mediation program and on your new job, it may be hard to imagine that you can be much help to anybody else. Although you probably cannot help much with information about the job, you may know other helpful things, such as the best place to get a haircut, or who makes the best pizza in town, or where the best parking spaces are. If you open up in that way to others, they are likely to open up to you. Over time, you will have enough knowledge about the job to be a mediation mentor; in the meantime, do what you can to create relationships.

Mentoring is not a one-way situation in which the senior person is helping the junior person along. Mentoring is multidirectional; it works best when those involved aim to advance themselves while looking out for one another. If a senior mediator is mentoring you and you hear about a job opening that is exactly what your mentor is looking for, you pass on that information. And the person mentoring you will be pleased to see you mentoring others. Nobody gets ahead without some help. Mentoring is a way of acknowledging this plain truth.

PROMOTING YOURSELF

There are still some people who are not sure just what a mediator does. (For instance, Shelley Rossoff Olson, Esq., a mediator for NAM, described being reviewed for a job on a judiciary panel and did not get it because the review board did not understand what she actually did.) When you are out at marketing events through your mediation company, make sure you discuss the process as a whole.

No matter how well you work with others and how organized you are, in the end you will be judged by the product you put out. You want to develop a reputation as someone who gets cases settled, does it right, and does it quickly.

Maintain a Record of Your Work

As your career progresses, find a way to keep track of the work you do. Please note that you should never make unauthorized copies of work to keep in your own personal file; doing so could lead to a breach in client confidentiality. But you can certainly keep a record of the cases you hear. On your calendar or elsewhere, write down the cases you were given, as well as when they were heard and how you handled them. This is a great way to track the path your career has taken, both for yourself and for your bosses.

Handle Criticism in a Positive Way

When you receive criticism about your job performance—and we all do at times—remain calm and listen carefully to what is being said. First, pay attention to positive comments. Most of us tend to zero in on the one bad thing and discount all the good. Let us say that your critique goes something like this: *Your research and preparation on this case were excellent; I do think you need to work a bit on your communication skills, however.* Do not walk away thinking, *My communication stinks!* Make sure you also register the part about your excellent research and preparation.

Second, ask for concrete help to rectify the situation. Instead of replying, *Thanks; I'll work on my communication*, ask for specific information. Is the problem your nonverbal communication, your word choices, your speech speed? Ask for suggestions. There are books on communication; or maybe you just need to remember the information you learned in your basic mediation training course. Then, follow the advice you are given and ask the person for help in the future. See if you can find a time when things are not so busy to ask for specific suggestions for changes.

SELF-EMPLOYMENT

As discussed earlier, working as a mediator can enable you to take that leap into self-employment. If you love building and growing a business, the idea of marketing and advertising, and the administrative side of business, you might want to look into being a sole proprietor. Working for yourself has many perks—you get to decide everything from how to decorate your office and what you should wear to how formal an environment you want to present. Of course, the downside is that every last decision, good or bad, ultimately rests on you.

MARKETING TECHNIQUES FOR THE SELF-EMPLOYED

1. **Define your services.** As you market yourself, make sure you clearly define what the process is because not everyone knows what mediation entails.

2. **Build trust.** Repeat such phrases as *confidentiality*, *voluntary participation*, *fair and balanced sessions*, *as the mediator, I am a neutral*, and *mutually acceptable agreements*. These concepts are central to the process and will help you gain your clients' trust.

3. **Offer value.** Sell your services within your niche. Market yourself as an expert mediator in one or a few specialized areas. Your clients will see the value in that. Contact the clients who will benefit from your specialty and make sure you have a presence with them.

4. **Use quality materials.** Develop professional, tasteful marketing materials. Design a logo that says something about your expertise and get it out into the community.

5. **Make lists of potential clients.** Keep lists of customers and companies that you think might be interested in your service. Mail them your marketing information and follow up with e-mails and phone calls. Keep updating your list with your progress and continue to add new names to it.

    Be persistent. It will take a good many e-mail, postal, and phone reminders before people remember who you are.

6. **Establish your niche.** Talk to other local mediators in the area. Ask them how they marketed themselves in the community. Position yourself differently from most of the other mediators in town and think about how what you do would benefit the community.

7. **Ask for referrals.** Ask for referrals from *everyone*—your neighbors, your friends, association members, your dentist, your doctor, your insurance agent, your plumber. And make sure you actively recommend your referral sources' services to others.

8. **Maximize your time at networking events.** Go to as many networking events as you can. Be sure to smile and greet everyone within reach.

    Wear businesslike attire and walk, talk, and behave like a professional.

    Before any networking event, put together a short introductory statement stating your name, your business name, and a few sentences explaining why someone should choose you to help settle their dispute.

    Take along your marketing material and business cards and distribute them liberally. Also, accept any business cards you are offered. Add these contacts to your list and send follow-up e-mails.

9. **Write a press release.** Write a few short paragraphs about something people do not know about mediation. Give the local newspaper a reason to print it and plug your business in the writeup.

10. **Get involved with community organizations.** Be an active member of the community. Give free talks to explain how mediation works to different community organizations. Join as many local organizations as you can. Work on volunteer or community projects for seniors, children, or abused women. Join a political group and get to know the political figures in your community or work with a philanthropic group. All of these activities will allow you to expand your contact list, become a known face in the community, and build trust in your business.

Getting Started

James Melamed, cofounder of Resourceful Internet Solutions (RIS) and Mediate.com, often suggests that new mediators print their stationery and cards and begin distributing them early on because they are unlikely to get a first-quality case for at least six months and they might as well get started.

One very important first step is to get to know the mediators and mediation service providers in the area, including the community mediation facilities and any state and local associations. You will also want to connect with the local courts to see what credentialing or experience you need in order to be referred cases. You might also scour the yellow pages to see how many other mediators there are in your area and ask them for advice on marketing and representing yourself in the community.

Make sure you are marketing yourself to the right audience. If you are a generalist, you will waste all your resources marketing all over the place. You need to establish an area of expertise that interests you and that you can build a reputation in. Then you need to figure out how best to target that particular audience.

Marketing

Once you have decided on a specialty, you want to make sure people know who you are. For instance, if you are a divorce mediator, start by targeting divorce layers and the matrimonial part in your local court. You might also leave your information with couples counselors in the community. It is vital that you get as much exposure as at all possible.

Get on the Internet
The Internet has quickly become one of the fastest and most cost-effective ways to market yourself. Select your e-mail address carefully. You might even invest in a professionally designed website. More people will find you on the Internet than through any other medium, so do not neglect this opportunity.

Send Out a Direct Mail Piece
Besides launching a website, consider sending out a large volume mailer. Make sure the mailer is printed on high-quality paper and that your marketing collateral is attractive, attention grabbing, and informative.

Your mailer should include a cover page introducing yourself and what you do, it should also include some kind of marketing material such as a brochure, to entice possible clients to use your services. You might want to include your resume. Finally, make sure you tell potential clients where they can reach you, whether by telephone or email or both.

Work with Your Responders
As you receive responses to your outreach efforts, make sure you organize and track them effectively. You can make follow-up calls, send out e-mails, or

ideally, try to set up face-to-face meetings so potential clients can get to know you on a more personal level.

Make Presentations

Another way to get yourself noticed is by speaking and making appearances as often as possible. If you have the opportunity to speak to a professional community group, do it! It will get you great exposure. Also, consider giving speeches or introductions at colleges, or even teaching mediation or continuing legal education classes.

Display Advertising

Yet another way to get exposure is with ads in your local newspapers. No need to place a huge spread in a national newspaper; just slowly but consistently let people know who you are and what you do. If you have a website, make sure your print ad directs potential clients to it.

Setting Fees for Your Services

Fees for mediation services vary, although they typically start at $50 an hour and can go all the way up $400 an hour. There is no strict formula for setting fees. Some mediators have disputants pay as they go, while others ask for a deposit, which is used toward the billed fees. Whichever method you choose, make sure you have a written agreement in place to ensure that all parties are clear about what their obligations are. Charging fees is important, as it can be used to encourage disputants to resolve their case as quickly as possible.

Inspire Trust

Trustworthiness is possibly the most important quality of a legal mediator. Mediators are entrusted with a great deal of responsibility. It is important that your clients feel they can trust you to be fair, impartial, and discreet. The parties in the dispute need to feel that you have their best interests at heart and will stand by them until their dispute is resolved. They should feel a personal connection to you. The process is most effective when the parties have a rapport with the mediator, a personal bond that allows them to feel they can really open up to the mediator about some difficult issues. The disputing parties also need to feel that you are fair to both disputants and that you are able to reason with both disputants in order to reach an agreement.

Cultivate Champions

Network, network, network! In order to build you practice, you need to create relationships with people who can help you become successful. These people might be other mediators or lawyers who might not know about the benefits of mediation. The ABA and various other legal associations hold regular dinners and networking events for people in the legal profession. If you can get just a few legal professionals to pass your name on to important clients and to large groups who may need your services, you will see a large payoff.

Practice Authenticity

Authenticity goes beyond honesty. Authenticity is the kind of truthfulness that comes from living a life of awareness and free of self-deception. For most of us, it is a personal and lifelong process. In mediation, authenticity means having the strength to work with uncertainties and the fears they bring every day. Often you have no idea where a case is going, or how to get it to where you want, but you must practice with authenticity in mind. This kind of practice is what will inspire people to trust you, to listen to your suggestions, and to come back to you when they have other disputes.

Create Value

Great mediators do everything they can to provide direction, support, and encouragement to their clients. They constantly try to come up with new tools to help clients solve problems.

Sometimes what is stopping resolution of a case is something as simple as wanting an apology. Jessica Lee Stockton, Esq., of NAM mentions an instance where a medical malpractice case turned because the doctor was willing to apologize. A mediator may have all the necessary skills—active listening, impartiality, problem solving skills—but every once in a while a new tool is necessary to solve a particular case. Building a reputation as someone who is able to do this will quickly make you particularly popular and build up your reputation as someone who has a particular knack for getting cases resolved.

Embrace Rejection

In mediation, you have to expect some rejection. There will always be several mediators vying for each case. If you do not get a particular case, you have to assume that the decision was not personal.

Practice the Three Ps

Building a successful mediation practice does not happen overnight. It takes patience, perseverance, and persistence. Your best bet is to relax and remind yourself that you have the skills it takes to succeed, that you are ready to be in the game long term, and that you will slowly but surely build up your practice. Nina Meierding, director and senior mediator at the Mediation Center in Ventura, California says, "My first year, I made $600. After four years, I was nowhere close to six figures. But I was also thinking, what is my goal? How much time and money am I going to invest before I reach six figures? You have to have an inordinate amount of patience. I haven't had a down month in ten years—it has been a very consistent, solid, respectable six-figure income for ten years."

Handling Emotional Overload

Some of the cases that you will hear as a mediator will be highly difficult emotionally—family cases where children are hurting, personal injury cases where someone has been crippled, or medical malpractice cases where someone has suffered terribly, to name a few. Hearing such cases can help you in your own progression as a human being, making you appreciate the wonderful things in your own life and be more compassionate in the way you treat others. Some of these cases are so terrible that you take them home with you and they may affect you after the mediation is done. Regardless of how terrible the case has been, you have to learn how to let it go and focus on the next case.

Standing Out in a Crowd

You may find that there are many mediators vying for the same mediation opportunities. In order to make yourself as marketable as possible, focus on what makes you unique. Think about how you can stand apart from others—it may mean teaching mediation workshops, publishing articles in the field, or consistently networking. Whatever you do, make sure people know your name.

Self-Marketing

In order to market yourself best as a mediator, you have to develop a reputation for being someone who mediates well and stays involved with the case until it is settled. You should also understand how to make others in the legal field see you as their peer. You may not want to wear conservative attire or behave in a way that makes you seem lawyerly, but you need to understand what people in your industry expect and behave and dress accordingly.

Staying Relevant

Mediators who are successful find ways to reinvent themselves constantly. Anyone can get stale after doing a job for a long time. In order to really excel in the field, you need to make sure that you are approaching every case with a fresh perspective for the disputing parties. When you find this becoming difficult, Eric Galton of Galtan, Cunningham, Bourgeois (GCB)

Mediators at the Lakeside Mediation Center in Texas recommends that you fix it fast by "acquiring and developing new techniques, hanging out at least twice a year with other mediators, and taking enough vacation time to recharge."

You might consider altering or trying new mediation techniques on for size. For example, perhaps you have been an avid user of the problem-solving approach, which requires that the disputants define their problems and then try to come up with possible solutions that they think might work for them both. One alternative technique is known as visioning. The goal here is to help parties identify shared goals. It is a way to get the parties away from talking about the problems they have and moving toward talking about shared goals.

Make sure you attend the legal professional associations dinners and other networking events; they will be attended by fellow mediators. Also, look to foster friendships and other casual relationships with other mediators who might be able to discuss different styles of mediation with you.

Even if you follow the guidelines above, you need to stay realistic in your expectations. You may not become a mediation success story the day after you enter the field. Most of your success will arise from building a reputation as an ethical, diligent mediator—and that kind of reputation builds up over time.

Also keep in mind, as you build up your practice, that your ultimate goal may not be to obtain the largest paycheck possible. As a mediator, you are changing how people approach their conflicts, how they communicate, and how they maintain their relationships. In essence, as a mediator, you are promoting peaceful resolutions to conflicts between people, which is truly a noble endeavor.

GOOD LUCK

As mentioned throughout this book, the mediation profession is growing, and does not look likely to slow down anytime soon. Not only are there more and more mediators, but they are also moving in many new directions and hearing many new types of cases. A career as a mediator can pay quite well, is well respected, and affords you opportunities for advancement. But the best thing about working in the mediation field is that regardless of the niche you are in or how routine your work may be, every day you make a huge difference in someone's life. It may be on a large scale (hearing environmental cases, international conflicts, or complex business disputes) or on a smaller scale (resolving disputes between an employer and an employee, or helping a child feel heard in a custody case, or making sure an injured party gets their fair share from an insurance company). These are only small victories in the grand scheme of things, but to your client they mean everything. And you helped make it happen.

THE INSIDE TRACK

What advice would you give an aspiring mediator?

Hon. John P. DiBlasi (Retired):

You must get training. Regardless of what the genre of cases you are hearing is, it is vital that you get training. This is a very specific process and you need to make sure you are well trained. Second, make sure you are well informed. There is a lot of great reading out there that you would benefit from. I continue to push myself to read about new techniques. One great book that I readily recommend is *Getting to Yes*. And finally, get some real experience by volunteering. There are lots of opportunities to do some local mediating by volunteering at the local courts and local agencies.

Jessica Lee Stockton, Esq.:

Be unique. When I'm hiring a mediator the uniqueness is a big part of what I look for. The difference between a superstar mediator and a mediocre one is often the personality. Some mediators have some trait that makes people come back to you. And market yourself. In a group like NAM, one of the benefits is that we triple your marketing. We attend as many American Bar Association and New York State Trial Lawyers Association function as possible to do our networking and marketing but it is a lot easier if I have the product, the mediator, there with me.

Mediation is really the wave of the future. In California it is used very readily. In New York where I'm working from now, it is not quite as popular yet, but it is slowly gaining more and more notoriety. Mediators I knew out in California could charge $8–10,000 per day!

How to Succeed Once You Have Landed the Job

Hon. Elizabeth Bonina:

I'm probably not the best person to answer this question. I got into it after so many years of legal work, I do not know what a young, aspiring mediator should do but I do know that it is an expanding profession. I see it becoming more and more mainstream every day.

Appendix A

Professional Associations and Organizations

BELOW YOU will find contact information for both national and state-specific legal mediation groups. Even though you are not yet a practicing legal mediator, it is not too early to start investigating organizations or associations in this field. This is a great opportunity to learn about the latest industry trends or to make professional contacts.

NATIONAL LEGAL MEDIATION ORGANIZATIONS

ACR Advanced Family Practioner
  (ACR AFP)
1015 18 Street NW, Suite 1150
Washington, DC 20036
Phone: 202-464-9700
Fax: 202-464-9720
E-mail: info@acrnet.org

American Arbitration Association
Corporate Headquarters
1633 Broadway, 10th Floor
New York, NY 10019
Phone: 212-716-5800
Fax: 212-716-5905
Website: www.adr.org

American Bar Association
321 N Clark Street
Chicago, IL 60654
Phone: 800-285-2221
E-mail: askaba@abanet.org
Website: www.abanet.org

American College of Civil Trial
   Mediators (ACCTM)
20 N Orange Avenue, Suite 704
Orlando, FL 32801
Phone: 407-843-8878
Fax: 407-843-1996
E-mail: acctm@acctm.org
Website: www.acctm.org

Association of Attorney-Mediators
PO Box 741955
Dallas, TX 75374
Phone: 800-280-1368
Fax: 972-669-8180
E-mail: aam@attorney-mediators.org
Website: www.attorney-mediators
   .org

Association for Conflict Resolution
2100 Sunset Hills Road, Suite 130
Reston, VA 20190
E-mail: membership@acrnet.org
Website: www.acrnet.org

Association of Family and Conciliation
6525 Grand Teton Plaza
Madison, WI 53719
Phone: 608-664-3750
Fax: 608-664-3751
E-mail: afcc@afccnet.org
Website: www.afccnet.org

Center for Resolution, LLC (CFR)
Offices throughout the United States
Phone: 866-922-2370
Fax: 312-264-0659
E-mail: mediate@centerforresolution
   .com
Website: www.cfrmediation.com

Conflict Resolution Center
314 Cambridge St Stop 8009
Grand Forks, ND 58202
Phone: 701-777-3664
Fax: 701-777-6182
E-mail: conflict_resolution@und.edu
Website: www.conflictresolution.und
   .edu

CoParenting Solutions, Inc.
214 Butler Road
Oak Ridge, TN 37830
Phone: 865-535-0037
E-mail: jkarney@gainagreement.com

Professional Associations and Organizations

Foreign Exchanges
8417 Waring Avenue
Los Angeles, CA 90069
Phone: 323-356-5003
E-mail: dorit@doritcypis.com
Website: www.doritcypis.com

National Arbitration and Mediation
990 Stewart Avenue
Garden City, NY 11530
Phone: 800-358-2550
Website: www.namadr.com

National Association for Community
    Mediation (NAFCM)
PO Box 44578
Madison, WI 53744
Phone: 608-845-9918
E-mail: nafcm@mailbag.com
Website: www.mediate.com/nafcm

National Center for State Courts
300 Newport Avenue
Williamsburg, VA 23185
Phone: 800-616-6164
Fax: 757-220-0449
Website: www.ncsc.org

STATE-SPECIFIC LEGAL MEDIATION ORGANIZATIONS

Alabama
Alabama Center for Dispute Resolution
PO Box 671
Montgomery, AL 36101
Phone: 334-269-0409
E-mail: jkeegan@alabar.org
Website: www.alabamaadr.org

Alaska
Alaska Dispute Settlement
    Organization
PO Box 242922
Anchorage, AK 99524
Phone: 907-258-0624

Arizona
Superior Court of Arizona—Alternative
    Dispute Resolution Department
Downtown Justice Center
650 W Jackson Street, Suite 3076
Phoenix, AZ 85003
Phone: 602-372-0240
E-mail: kphilips@superiorcourt
    .maricopa.gov

Arkansas
Arkansas ADR Commission
Justice Building
625 Marshall Street, Suite 1100
Little Rock, AR 72207
Phone: 501-682-9400

California

Southern California Mediation Association
1430 South Grand Avenue, #256
Glendora, CA 91740
Phone: 877-963-3428
Fax: 626-974-5439
Website: www.scmediation.org

Colorado

Colorado Council of Mediators and Mediation Organizations (CCMO)
PO Box 11696
Denver, CO 80211
Phone: 303-322-9275, 800-864-4317
E-mail: ccmo@coloradomediation.org
Website: www.coloradomediation.org

Connecticut

Connecticut Council for Divorce Mediation and Collaborative Practice (CCDM)
Phone: 888-236-2236
E-mail: info@ctmediators.org
Website: www.ctmediators.org

Delaware

Superior Court of Delaware—ADR
38 The Green
Dover, DE 19901
Phone: 302-739-8431

District of Columbia

Superior Court of the District of Columbia
Multi-Door Courthouse Division
515 5 Street, NW
Washington, DC 20001
Phone: 202-879-1549

Florida

Florida Circuit-Civil Mediator Society (FCCMS)
2701 W Busch Boulevard
Tampa, FL 33618
Phone: 813-600-5678
Fax: 813-257-4698
E-mail: admin@floridamediators.org
Website: www.floridamediators.org

Georgia

Georgia Office of Dispute Resolution
244 Washington Street SW, Suite 423
Atlanta, GA 30354
Phone: 404-463-3788

Hawaii

The Center for Alternative Dispute Resolution
Ali'iolani Hale
417 South King Street, Room 207
Honolulu, HI 96813
Phone: 808-539-4237

Professional Associations and Organizations

Idaho
Supreme Court Building
451 West State Street
PO Box 83720
Boise, ID 83720
Phone: 208-334-2246

Illinois
Resolution Systems Institute
11 E Adams Street, Suite 500
Chicago, IL 60603
Phone: 312-922-6475 x924
Fax: 312-922-6463
E-mail: info@aboutrsi.org

Indiana
The Mediation Group, LLC
8888 Keystone Crossing, Suite 1500
Indianapolis, IN 46240
Phone: 317-569-3000
Website: www.mede8-com

Iowa
Iowa Association of Mediators
8710 Earhart Lane SW
Cedar Rapids, IA 52402
Phone: 319-841-5151
E-mail: sovern@mediate.com
Website: www.iamediators.org

Kansas
Kansas Office of Judicial Administration
301 W Tenth Street, Room 337
Topeka, KS 66612
Phone: 785-291-3748

Kentucky
Kentucky Administrative Office of the Courts
100 Millcreek Park
Frankfort, KY 40601
Phone: 502-573-2350

Louisiana
Deputy Judicial Administrator/General Counsel
Supreme Court of Louisiana
1555 Poydras Street, Suite 1540
New Orleans, LA 70112
Phone: 504-568-5740

Maine
Court ADR Service of the State of Maine
Judicial Branch
RR1 Box 310
West Bath, ME 04530
Phone: 207-442-0227

Maryland
Maryland Council for Dispute Resolution
8288 Telegraph Road, Suite A
Odenton, MD 21113
Phone: 410-672-2237
E-mail: mcdr_a@yahoo.com

Massachusetts

Massachusetts Council of Family
  Mediation
PO Box 59
Ashland, NH 03217
Phone: 781-449-4430
E-mail: masscouncil@mcfm.org
Website: www.mcfm.org

Michigan

Michigan State Court Administrative
  Office
Office of Dispute Resolution
309 N Washington Square
PO Box 30048
Lansing, MI 48909
Phone: 517-373-4839

Minnesota

Mediation Services of Minnesota, Inc.
1107 Hershey Street
Albert Lea, MN 56007
Phone: 507-373-4842
Fax: 507-373-0038
E-mail: llbottel@smig.net

Mississippi

Administrative Office of the Courts
PO Box 117
Jackson, MS 39205-0117
Phone: 601-354-7449

Missouri

Association of Missouri Mediators
  (AMM)
PO Box 2257
Jefferson City, MO 65102
Phone: 816-736-8402
Fax: 816-736-8401
E-mail: momediators@mediate.com
Website: www.mediate.com/amm

Center for Dispute Resolution, Missouri
  State
Missouri State University
901 S National
Springfield, MO 65897
Phone: 417-836-8831
Fax: 417-836-8288
E-mail: cdr@missouristate.edu

Montana

Montana Mediation Association
PO Box 6363
Great Falls, MT 59406
Phone: 406-727-8365
E-mail: memberservices@mtmediation
  .org
Website: www.mtmediation.org

Nebraska

Nebraska Office of Dispute Resolution
Administrative Office of the
  Courts/Probation
State Capitol Building, Room 1207
PO Box 98910
Lincoln, NE 68509
Phone: 402-471-3148

Professional Associations and Organizations

Nebraska Mediation Center
   Association
PO Box 295
Eagle, NE 68347
Phone: 402-781-2011

Nevada
Family Mediation and Assessment
   Center
Family Court and Services Center
601 North Pecos Road
Las Vegas, NV 89101
Phone: 702-455-4186

Family Mediation Program
Courthouse
75 Court Street
Reno, NV 89501
Phone: 775-328-3556

New Hampshire
Superior Court ADR Committee
22 Main Street
Newport, NH 03773
Phone: 603-863-3450

New Jersey
New Jersey Mediation Group, LLC
601 Ewing Street, C-14
Princeton, NJ 08540
Phone: 609-275-1352

New Mexico
New Mexico Mediation Association
PO Box 82384
Albuquerque, NM 87198
Phone: 505-466-1804

New York
New York State Dispute Resolution
   Association (NYSDRA)
255 River Street
Troy, NY 12180
Phone: 518-687-2240
Fax: 518-687-2245
E-mail: noe-mail_info@nysdra.org
Website: www.nysdra.org

North Carolina
Mediation Network of North Carolina
   (MNNC)
PO Box 648
215 S Fir Avenue
Siler City, NC 27344
Phone: 919-663-5650
Fax: 919-663-5650
E-mail: mnnc@mnnc.org
Website: www.mediate.com/mnnc

North Dakota
State Bar Association of North Dakota
PO Box 2136
Bismarck, ND 58502
Phone: 701-255-1404

Ohio

Mediation Association of NE Ohio
(MANO)
8508 Eaton Drive
Sagamore Hills, OH 44067
Phone: 440-354-1400
E-mail: mennesm@aol.com

Ohio Mediation Association (OMA)
2897 Liberty Bell Lane
Reynoldsburg, OH 43068
Phone: 614-863-4775
Fax: 614-863-4775
E-mail: omapresident@mediateohio.org
Website: www.mediate.com/ohio

Oklahoma

Oklahoma Academy of Mediators and
Arbitrators
13308 N MacArthur Boulevard
Oklahoma City, OK 73142
Phone: 405-443-5656
E-mail: info@oama.org

Oklahoma Agricultural Mediation
Program (OAMP)
1514 West Hall of Fame
Stillwater, OK 73034
Phone: 800-248-5465
Fax: 405-744-3050
E-mail:
andrea.braeutigam@okstate.edu
Website: www.ok.gov/mediation

Oregon

Oregon Mediation Association (OMA)
PO Box 40041
Portland, OR 97240
Phone: 503-872-9775
Fax: 503-245-5998
E-mail: oma@omediate.org
Website: www.mediate.com/oma

Pennsylvania

Pennsylvania Council of Mediators
Center for Alternatives in Community
Justice
411 S Burrowes Street
State College, PA 16801
Phone: 814-234-1059

Rhode Island

Rhode Island Mediators Association
9 Juniper Court
Bristol, RI 02809
Phone: 401-253-2458
E-mail: info@rimediators.org
Website: www.rimediators.org

South Carolina

Public Services Counsel
South Carolina Bar
950 Taylor Street
PO Box 608
Columbia, SC 29202
Phone: 803-799-4015

Professional Associations and Organizations

South Dakota
Dakota Counseling and Mediation
1801 E. Kemp Avenue
Watertown, SD 57201
Phone: 605-753-5520

Tennessee
The Mediation Group of Tennessee, LLC
2809 Wimbledon Road
Nashville, TN 37215
Phone: 615-292-6069

Texas
Texas Association of Mediators
PO Box 2537
Galveston, TX 77553
Website: www.txmediator.org

Utah
Utah Council on Conflict Resolution (UCCR)
PO Box 521656
Salt Lake City, UT 84152
Phone: 801-685-8227
Fax: 801-281-9675
E-mail: info@uccr.net
Website: www.uccr.net

Vermont
Office of State Court Administrator
109 State Street
Montpelier, VT 05609
Phone: 802-828-3276

Virginia
Virginia Mediation Network (VMN)
2231 Oak Bay Lane
Richmond, VA 23233
Phone: 804-254-2666
E-mail: office@vamediation.org
Website: www.vamediation.org

Washington
Washington Mediation Association
PMB 1095
1122 E Pike Street
Seattle, WA 98122
Phone: 509-735-3619
E-mail: dpuls@charter.net
Website: www.washingtonmediation.org

West Virginia
Kanawha County Magistrate Court Mediation
Building 1, Room E-100
1900 Kanawha Boulevard E
Charleston, WV 25309
Phone: 304-558-0145

Wisconsin
Medical Mediation Panels
110 E Main Street, Room 320
Madison, WI 53703
Phone: 608-266-7711

Wyoming
Supreme Court Building
2301 Capital Avenue
Cheyenne, WY 82002
Phone: 307-777-7581

Appendix B

Legal Mediation Training Programs

BELOW ARE listings for mediation training programs available in different states. Although education in conflict resolution isn't mandatory in order to practice as a mediator, you'll find programs like these useful when starting out in this industry.

Alabama
Alabama Center for Dispute
 Resolution
PO Box 671
Montgomery, AL 36101
Phone: 334-269-0409

Alaska
Alaska Dispute Settlement Association
PO Box 242922
Anchorage, AK 99524
Phone: 907-258-0624

Arizona

The Community Mediation Program
c/o Our Town Family Center
3830 E Bellevue Street
Tucson, AZ 85716
Phone: 520-323-7862
Website: www.otfc.org

Arkansas

Arkansas Conflict Management, Inc
1501 N University Avenue, Suite 568
Little Rock, AR 72207
Phone: 501-681-1357

California

Center for Peacemaking and Conflict
  Studies of Fresno
1717 S Chestnut
Fresno, CA 93702
E-mail: pacs@fresno.edu
Website: www.peace.fresno.edu

CONCUR, Inc.
1832 Second Street
Berkeley, CA 94710
Phone: 510-649-8008
E-mail: info@concurinc.net
Website: www.concurinc.com

Mediation Offices of Steven Rosenberg
775 East Blithedale Avenue, #363
Mill Valley, CA 94941
Phone: 415-383-5544
E-mail: steven@rosenbergmediation
  .com
Website: www.rosenbergmediation
  .com

Mosten Mediation Training
11661 San Vicente Boulevard, Suite
  1010
Los Angeles, CA 90049
Phone: 310-473-7611
E-mail: jodym@mostenmediation.com
Website: www.mostenmediation.com

Northern California Mediation Center
175 North Redwood Drive, Suite 295
San Rafael, CA 94903
Phone: 415-461-6392
E-mail: njfoster@ncmc-mediate.org
Website: www.ncmc-mediate.org

Straus Institute for Dispute Resolution
24255 Pacific Coast Highway
Malibu, CA 90263
Phone: 310-506-4655
E-mail: dracademics@law.pepperdine
  .edu
Website: www.law.pepperdine.edu/
  straus/

Legal Mediation Training Programs

Win Win Training and Mediation
22647 Ventura Boulevard, Suite 422
Woodland Hills, CA 91364
Phone: 818-347-5098
E-mail: barb@winwintraining.com
Website: www.winwintraining.com

Colorado

Mediators without Borders
4450 Arapahoe Avenue, Suite 100
Boulder, CO 80303
Phone: 877-268-5337
E-mail: information@mediatorswithout
   borders.com
Website: http://www.mediatorswithout
   borders.org

Jefferson County Mediation Services
700 Jefferson County Parkway,
   Suite 220
Golden, CO 80401
Phone: 303-271-5060

Connecticut

American Arbitration Association
111 Founders Plaza, 17th Floor
East Hartford, CT 06108
Phone: 860-289-3993
Website: www.adr.org

Dispute Settlement Center, Inc.
134 Old Ridgefield Road
Wilton, CT 06897
Phone: 203-831-8012
Website: www.ctresolution.org

Community Mediation, Inc.
32 Elm Street
New Haven, CT 06510
Phone: 203-782-3500
Website: www.community-mediation
   .org

Delaware

Creative Learning Solutions, Inc.
109 Chapel Hill Drive
Newark, DE 19711
Phone: 302-738-4173

University of Delaware
Conflict Resolution Program
177 Graham Hall
Newark, DE 19716
Phone: 302-831-8158
Website: www.ipa.udel.edu/topics/
   conflict-res.html

Victim Restoration and Community
   Mediation Program
100 W 10th Street, Suite 905
Wilmington, DE 19801
Phone: 302-658-7273

District of Columbia

Center for Dispute Settlement
1666 Connecticut Avenue, NW
Washington, DC 20009
Phone: 202-265-9572
E-mail: administrator@cdsusa.org
Website: www.cdsusa.org

Becoming a LEGAL MEDIATOR

School of International Service:
  Peacebuilding and Development
  Institute
4400 Massachusetts Avenue, NW
Washington, DC 20016
Phone: 202-885-2112
E-mail: pcrinst@american.edu
Website: www1.sis.american.edu/
  peacebuilding

Florida

Nova Southeastern University
3301 College Avenue
Ft. Lauderdale, FL 33314
Phone: 800-986-6529
E-mail: admission@nsu.law.nova.edu
Website: www.nova.edu

Perry S. Itkin, Esq.
Dispute Resolution, Inc.
2200 NE 33 Avenue, Suite 8G
Fort Lauderdale, FL 33305
Phone: 954-567-9746
Website: www.mediationtrainingcenter
  .com

USF Conflict Resolution Collaborative
2901 W Busch Boulevard, Suite 707
Tampa, FL 33618
Phone: 800-852-5362
Website: www.cme.hsc.usf.edu

Georgia

Atlantic Divorce Mediators, Inc
150 E Ponce de Leon Avenue,
  Suite 220
Decatur, GA 30030
Phone: 404-378-3238

Justice Center of Atlanta
976 Edgewood Avenue NE
Atlanta, GA 30307
Phone: 404-523-8236
Website: www.justicecenter.org

Hawaii

Clay Chapman Iwamure Pulice &
  Nervell
700 Bishop Street, Suite 2100
Honolulu, HI 96813
Phone: 808-535-8400
Website: www.paclawteam.com

Mediation Services of Maui, Inc.
95 Mahalani Street, Suite 25
Wailuku, HI 96793
Phone: 808-244-5744

Idaho

Northwest Institute for Dispute
  Resolution
Sixth and Rayburn Street
Moscow, ID 83844
Phone: 208-885-4977

Legal Mediation Training Programs

Illinois

Northwestern University
3639 E Chicago Avenue
Chicago, IL 60611
Phone: 312-503-8583
E-mail: n-flowers@law.northwestern.edu
Website: www.northwestern.edu

Center for Conflict Resolution
11 East Adams Street, Suite 500
Chicago, IL 60603
Phone: 312-922-6464
Website: www.ccrchicago.org

Indiana

Indiana Continuing Legal Education
   Forum
230 E Ohio Street, Suite 333
Indianapolis, IN 46204
Phone: 317-637-9102
Website: www.iclef.org

Community Conflict Resolution
   Program, Inc.
PO Box 6282
Bloomington, IN 47407
Phone: 812-855-1618

Iowa

Sovern Mediation, LLC
Resolution Center
8710 Earhart Lane SW
Cedar Rapids, IA 52404
Phone: 319-841-5151
E-mail: sovern@mediate.com
Website: www.mediate.com/steve
   sovern

Community Mediation Center
Family Resources, Inc.
805 W 35 Street, Suite 100
Davenport, IA 52806
Phone: 563-445-0557
Website: www.famres.org

Iowa Mediation Service
1025 Ashworth Road, Suite 504
West Des Moines, IA 50265
Phone: 515-331-8081
Website: www.mediation-service.com

Kansas

Mediation Training Institute
   International
5700 W 79 Street
Prairie Village, KS 66208
Phone: 888-222-3271
E-mail: info@mediationworks.com
Website: www.mediationworks.com

Counseling and Mediation Center
2082 Westridge Court
Wichita, KS 67203
Phone: 316-943-2066

Mediation Center, Inc.
6405 Metcalf Avenue
Overland Park, KS 66202
Phone: 913-831-4202

Kentucky

The International Center for Dispute
    Resolution Leadership
3101 Bardstown Road
Louisville, KY 40205
Phone: 502-456-0019

Just Solutions
410 W Chestnut Street, Suite 628
Louisville, KY 40202
Phone: 502-581-1961
Website: www.just-solutions.org

Louisiana

Turning Point Partners
1137 Baronne Street
New Orleans, LA 70113
Phone: 504-620-5138
Website: www.turningpointpartners
    .com

Family and Educational Services
6031 Perrier Street
New Orleans, LA 70118
Phone: 504-895-4355
Website: www.familymediationcouncil
    .com

Maine

Sweetser Institute
50 Moody Street
Saco, ME 04072
Phone: 800-434-3000
Website: www.sweetser.org

University of Southern Maine
Center for Continuing Education
Mediation—Basic and Advanced
    Training
68 High Street
Portland, ME 04101
Phone: 207-780-5900
Website: www.usm.maine.edu/cce

Maryland

Community Mediation Program, Inc.
3333 Greenmount Avenue
Baltimore, MD 21218
Phone: 410-467-9165

Rockville Community Mediation
    Program
City Hall
111 Maryland Avenue
Rockville, MD 20850
Phone: 301-309-3308
Website: www.ci.rockville.md.us

Massachusetts

The Negotiating Table
One Broadway, Suite 600
Cambridge, MA 02446
Phone: 617-577-0101
Website: www.negotiatingtable.com

Legal Mediation Training Programs

WCAC, Inc.
Community Mediation Center
484 Main Street, Second Floor
Worcester, MA 01608
Phone: 508-754-1176

Michigan

Zena Zumeta
Mediation Training and Consultation
　　Institute
330 E Liberty, Suite 3A
Ann Arbor, MI 48104
Phone: 800-535-1155
E-mail: info@learn2mediate.com
Website: www.learn2mediate.com

Western UP Mediators
115 East Ayer Street
Ironwood, MI 49938
Phone: 906-932-0070

Community Mediation Services
116 Fifth Street
Gaylord, MI 49735
Phone: 989-732-1576

Minnesota

North Hennepin Mediation Program,
　　Inc.
3300 County Road 10, Suite 212
Brooklyn Center, MN 55429
Phone: 763-561-0033
Website: www.mediationprogram.com

Twin Cities Mediation
790 Cleveland Avenue S, Suite 204
St. Paul, MN 55116
Phone: 612-824-8988
Website: http://twincitiesmediation
　　.com

Mississippi

The Accord Institute
PO Box 1396
Olive Branch, MS 38654
Phone: 417-872-8374

Missouri

Missouri State University
901 S National
Springfield, MO 65897
Phone: 417-836-5000
E-mail: info@missouristate.edu
Website: www.missouristate.edu

University of Missouri–Columbia
206 Hulston Hall
Columbia, MO 65211
Phone: 573-882-5969
E-mail: umclawcdr@missouri.edu
Website: www.law.missouri.edu/csdr

Montana

Community Mediation Center
104 East Main Street, Suite 312
Bozeman, MT 59715
Phone: 406-522-8442
Website: www.communitymediation
　　.com

Montana Mediators
PO Box 159
Missoula, MT 59806
Phone: 406-543-1113
Website: www.montanamediate.com/home.htm

Nebraska
Concord Center
3861 Farnam Street, Suite B
Omaha, NE 68131
Phone: 402-345-1131
Website: www.concord-center.com

Resolution Center
5109 West Scott Road, Suite 414
Beatrice, NE 68310
Phone: 402-223-6061

Nevada
Neighborhood Mediation Center
124 Ridge Street
Reno, NV 89501
Phone: 775-788-2127
Website: www.mediatenmc.org

New Hampshire
Cheshire Mediation
64 Main Street
Keene, NH 03431
Phone: 603-357-6873
Fax: 603-352-5698
Website: cheshiremediation.org

Roundtable Mediation and Conflict Management Consultants
670 North Commercial Street
Manchester, NH 03101
Phone: 603-623-3500
Website: www.roundtablemediation.com

Rose Hill Mediation Center
87 Deer Run Lane
Northwood, NH 03261
Phone: 603-942-8363

New Jersey
Community Mediation Services, Inc.
1201 Bacharach Boulevard, Third Floor
Atlantic City, NJ 08401
Phone: 609-345-7267

New Mexico
Mediation Services of New Mexico
PO Box 359
Corrales, NM 87048
Phone: 505-867-6550

New York
Center for Mediation and Training
111 W 90 Street
New York, NY 10024
Phone: 212-799-4302
Website: www.divorcemediation.com

Legal Mediation Training Programs

College of Criminal Justice
899 Tenth Avenue
New York, NY 10019
Phone: 212-237-8692
Website: www.johnjay.jjay.cuny.edu/dispute

CPR® International Institute for Conflict Prevention and Resolution
575 Lexington Avenue, 21st Floor
New York, NY 10022
Phone; 212-949-6490
Website: www.cpradr.org

North Carolina
Mediation Center of Eastern Carolina
PO Box 4428
Greenville, NC 27836
Phone: 252-758-0268
Website: www.mceconline.org

The Mediation Center
189 College Street
Asheville, NC 28801
Phone: 828-251-6089
Website: www.main.nu.us/tmc

North Dakota
University of North Dakota
Conflict Resolution Center
314 Cambridge Street Stop 8009
Grand Forks, ND 58202
Phone: 701-777-3664
Website: http://conflictresolution.und.edu

Ohio
Community Mediation Center of Stark County
222 Market N, Suite 122
Canton, OH 44702
Phone: 330-458-2088

Village Mediation Program
100 Dayton Street
Yellow Springs, OH 45387
Phone: 937-268-4830
Website: www.yso.com/vmp.asp

Oklahoma
Early Settlement Northwest
Major County Courthouse
Fairview, OK 73737
Phone: 580-227-2711

Oregon
Robert D. Benjamin, JD
Mediation and Conflict Management Services
3246 SW Cascade Terrace
Portland, OR 97201
Phone: 503-417-2655
Website: www.rbenjamin.com

University of Oregon School of Law
Appropriate Dispute Resolution Center
1515 Agate Street
Eugene, OR 97403
Phone: 541-346-3042
E-mail: broadous@uoregon.edu
Website: http://www.law.uoregon.edu

Pennsylvania

Good Shepherd Mediation Program
5356 Chew Avenue
Philadelphia, PA 19138
Phone: 215-843-5413
Website: www.phillymediators.org

Montgomery County Mediation Center
26 West Main Street
Norristown, PA 19401
Phone: 610-277-8909

Rhode Island

Community Mediation Center of Rhode Island
570 Broad Street
Providence, RI 02907
Phone: 401-273-9999

Mediation Consultants, Inc.
72 Pine Street
Providence, RI 02903
Phone: 401-272-5300

South Carolina

USC Spartanburg
Center for Mediation and Conflict Resolution
800 University Way
Spartanburg, SC 29303
Phone: 864-503-5631

Community Mediation Center
PO Box 5942
Columbia, SC 29250
Phone: 803-714-1176
Website: www.midnet.sc.edu/mediation

Tennessee

Lipscomb University Institute for Conflict Management
3901 Granny White Pike
Nashville, TN 37204
Phone: 800-333-4358
Website: http//icm.lipscomb.edu/

The Mediation Center
104 W 7 Street, Suite B
Columbia, TN 38401
Phone: 931-840-5583
Website: www.tmc-columbia.org

Texas

Southern Methodist University Dispute Resolution Program
5228 Tennyson Parkway
Plano, TX 75024
Phone: 973-473-3435
E-mail: kbarclay@smu.edu
Website: www.smu.edu/education/disputeresolution

Legal Mediation Training Programs

Center for Public Policy Dispute
    Resolution
727 East Dean Keeton Street
Austin, TX 78705
Phone: 512-471-3507
Website: www.utexas.edu/law/cppdr

Utah
The Community Mediation Center
800 West University Parkway
Orem, UT 84058
Phone: 801-863-7917
Website: www.communitymediation
    center.org

Utah Dispute Resolution
645 South 200 East
Salt Lake City, UT 84111
Phone: 801-532-4841
Website: www.utahdisputeresolution
    .org

Vermont
Champlain College
163 S Willard Street
Burlington, VT 05402
Phone: 802-860-2700
E-mail: admission@champlain.edu
Website: www.champlain.edu

Woodstock Institute for Negotiation
Pomfret Stage Road, Drawer 29
Woodstock, VT 05091
Phone: 802-457-3211
Website: www.woodstockinstitute.com

Virginia
Community Mediation Center
586 Virginian Drive
Norfolk, VA 23505
Phone: 757-480-2777
Website: www.conflictcrushers.org

Mediation Center of Hampton Roads
424 W 21 Street
Norfolk, VA 23517
Phone: 757-624-6666
E-mail: www.mediationhamptonroads
    .com

Washington
Eastern Washington University
Certificate in Conflict Management
Patterson 362, M-S174, 526 Fifth
    Avenue
Cheney, WA 99004
Phone: 509-359-6246

Benton Franklin Dispute Resolution
    Center
5219 W Clearwater Avenue, Suite 11
Kennewick, WA 99336
Phone: 509-783-3325
Website: www.bfdrc.org

West Virginia
West Virginia Center for Dispute
    Resolution
55 Don Knotts Boulevard
Morgantown, WV 26508
Phone: 304-296-2124

Wisconsin

Wisconsin Association of Mediators
PO Box 44578
Madison, WI 53744
Phone: 608-848-1970
E-mail: wam@mailbag.com
Website: www.wamediators.org

Wyoming

Center for Resolution
PO Box 13691
Jackson, WY 83002
Phone: 307-734-6620

Appendix C

Additional Resources

NOW THAT you have a sense of the steps you need to take to accomplish your educational and career goals, look through this appendix for sources that will give you more specific advice on the area with which you need help.

The resources listed here will help you delve deeper into the topics covered in this book.

GENERAL INFORMATION

Bush, Robert A. Baruch, and Joseph P. Folger. *The Promise of Mediation: The Transformative Approach to Conflict.* San Francisco: Jossey-Bass, 2005.

Lovenheim, Peter, and Emily Doskow. *Becoming a Mediator: Your Guide to Career Opportunities.* Berkeley: Nolo, 2004.

Moore, Christopher W. *The Mediation Process: Practical Strategies for Resolving Conflict.* San Francisco: Jossey-Bass, 2003.

Nolan-Haley, Jacqueline M. *Alternative Dispute Resolution.* 3rd ed. Eagan, Minnesota: Thomson/West, 1992.

FINDING A JOB

Job Interviews That Get You Hired. New York: LearningExpress, 2006.

McKinney, Anne, ed. *Real Resumes for Legal and Paralegal Jobs.* Fayetteville, NC: Prep Publishing, 2004.

Resumes That Get You Hired. New York: LearningExpress, 2006.

SUCCESS ON THE JOB

Garner, Bryan A., ed. *Black's Law Dictionary*, 9th ed. Boston: Houghton Mifflin, 2006.

The Bluebook: A Uniform System of Citation, 18th ed. Harvard Law Review Association, 1996.

Burton, William C. *Burton's Legal Thesaurus*, 3rd ed. New York: McGraw-Hill, 2001.

Garner, Bryan A. *The Elements of Legal Style*, 2nd ed. New York: Oxford University Press, 2002.

WEBSITES

American Arbitration Association: www.adr.org
American Bar Association: www.abanet.org
The Association for Conflict Resolution: www.acrenet.org
FindLaw: www.findlaw.com
Guide to Law Online: www.loc.gov/law/guide
Jurist Legal News and Research: www.jurist.law.pitt.edu
Law.com: www.law.com

Additional Resources

Law Guru: www.lawguru.com
Legal Engine: www.legalengine.com
Mediate.com—Everything Mediation: www.mediate.com
Nolo: www.nolo.com/statute/index.cfm/LR.index.html

Appendix D

Glossary of Legal Terms

action. A civil judicial proceeding whereby one party prosecutes another for a wrong done or for protection of a right or prevention of a wrong; requires service of process on adversary party or potentially adversary party.

adversary. The opponent in a case.

adversary system. The system of trial practice in the United States and some other countries in which each of the opposing, or adversary, parties has full opportunity to present and establish its opposing contentions before the court.

alternative dispute resolution (ADR). Ways to resolve a conflict without going to court. Mediation and arbitration are examples of alternative dispute resolution.

appeal. A proceeding to have a case examined by an appropriate higher court to see whether a lower court's decision was made correctly according to law.

arbitration. A formal process of conflict resolution that uses one or more neutrals to listen to evidence and render a decision. The decision may be binding or nonbinding.

attorney. A person who is trained to represent others in legal matters; a lawyer.

bench trial. A trial without a jury. The judge decides the outcome of the case.

binding. Legally enforceable. Court decisions are binding.

civil case or **civil suit.** A lawsuit that does not involve a criminal matter and usually involves monetary damages to gain repayment for a wrong.

commercial mediation. Mediation used in commercial disputes; for example, where the disputing parties are two companies.

community mediation. Mediation applied to deal with conflict between individuals and/or groups in the community.

complainant. A person who expresses a problem.

complaint. A document filed to begin a legal case.

conciliation. The use of a third person who is asked to help people reach an amicable resolution of their dispute. The conciliator attempts to resolve the differences between the parties by lowering tensions, helping them to communicate, and helping them to explore potential solutions. The conciliator does not have the authority to impose a settlement and usually speaks with the parties separately.

conflict management. Long-term management of disputes used to control and/or prevent random violence.

conflict resolution. A permanent resolution that has been established by addressing the needs of both parties.

conflict resolution process. The wide range of methods and processes by which conflicts are alleviated or resolved.

consensus. A decision that has been agreed to by everyone it pertains to.

consent order. A settlement agreed upon and signed by a judge in the form of a court order.

contract. A legally enforceable agreement between two or more parties.

criminal case. A case brought by the government against a person accused of violating criminal laws.

defense attorney. The lawyer who defends the defendant or the accused person.

Glossary of Legal Terms

defendant. The accused person, the person against whom charges are being brought.

disputing parties. The parties (individuals, corporations, or other legal entities) that are involved in a conflict.

docket. A list of documents in a case that have been filed with the clerk's office; the court's caseload.

evidence. Legally relevant pieces of proof used to convince the court or a jury.

facilitation. A process through which a neutral party helps members of a group to define and meet their goals, exchange ideas and information, solve a problem, or hold effective meetings.

impartiality. Approaching a situation or confrontation with a neutral mind-set.

judgment. The final appealable order in a civil or criminal case.

jurisdiction. The authority the court has to act or hear a case or make a decision.

jury trial. A trial in which a jury hears the facts of a case and gives a decision.

liability. A legal responsibility.

liable. Legally responsible.

litigants. The parties involved in a lawsuit.

litigation. A legal dispute argued in court. The disputants have little control over the process or the outcome.

mediation. A method for discussing problems and exploring solutions with the help of a trained neutral—the mediator. Mediators do not take sides, give legal advice, make decisions about resolutions, or impose solutions.

mediator. A trained professional who works to help others with their disputes, ultimately assisting with their overall resolution.

negotiation. A discussion between two or more parties in order to resolve a dispute, decide on an action, or make a bargain. A negotiation may involve advocates or representatives.

party. One side in a lawsuit.

petition. A formal written request made to a court.

plaintiff. The party who starts a lawsuit.

resolution-resistant conflict. Confrontations that are extremely difficult to resolve.

settlement agreement. A signed document establishing the overall terms agreed upon during the mediation, which both parties consent to abide by.

statute of limitations. A legally established time limit for starting a lawsuit.

Supreme Court. The highest court in a state and the highest court in the country.

verdict. A formal decision made by a jury or a judge.

witness. One who testifies in court under oath as to what he or she saw or heard or otherwise has knowledge about.

Appendix E

Model Standards of Conduct for Mediators

The *Model Standards of Conduct for Mediators* was prepared in 1994 by the American Arbitration Association, the American Bar Association's Section of Dispute Resolution, and the Association for Conflict Resolution.[1] A joint committee consisting of representatives from the same successor organizations revised the Model Standards in 2005.[2] Both the original 1994 version and the 2005 revision have been approved by each participating organization.[3]

---

[1] The Association for Conflict Resolution is a merged organization of the Academy of Family Mediators, the Conflict Resolution Education Network, and the Society of Professionals in Dispute Resolution (SPIDR). SPIDR was the third participating organization in the development of the 1994 Standards.

[2] Reporter's Notes, which are not part of these Standards and therefore have not been specifically approved by any of the organizations, provide commentary regarding these revisions.

[3] Proposed language. As of April 10, 2005, no organization has reviewed or approved the 2005 Revision.

Preamble

Mediation is used to resolve a broad range of conflicts within a variety of settings. These Standards are designed to serve as fundamental ethical guidelines for persons mediating in all practice contexts. They serve three primary goals: to guide the conduct of mediators; to inform the mediating parties; and to promote public confidence in mediation as a process for resolving disputes.

Mediation is a process in which an impartial third party facilitates communication and negotiation and promotes voluntary decision making by the parties to the dispute.

Mediation serves various purposes, including providing the opportunity for parties to define and clarify issues, understand different perspectives, identify interests, explore and assess possible solutions, and reach mutually satisfactory agreements, when desired.

Note on Construction

These Standards are to be read and construed in their entirety. There is no priority significance attached to the sequence in which the Standards appear.

The use of the term "shall" in a Standard indicates that the mediator must follow the practice described. The use of the term "should" indicates that the practice described in the standard is highly desirable, but not required, and is to be departed from only for very strong reasons and requires careful use of judgment and discretion.

The use of the term "mediator" is understood to be inclusive so that it applies to co-mediator models.

These Standards do not include specific temporal parameters when referencing a mediation, and therefore, do not define the exact beginning or ending of a mediation.

Various aspects of a mediation, including some matters covered by these Standards, may also be affected by applicable law, court rules, regulations, other applicable professional rules, mediation rules to which the parties have agreed and other agreements of the parties. These sources may create conflicts with, and may take precedence over, these Standards. However, a mediator should make every effort to comply with the spirit and intent of these Standards in resolving such conflicts. This effort should include honoring all remaining Standards not in conflict with these other sources.

These Standards, unless and until adopted by a court or other regulatory authority do not have the force of law. Nonetheless, the fact that these Standards have been

Model Standards of Conduct for Mediators

adopted by the respective sponsoring entities, should alert mediators to the fact that the Standards might be viewed as establishing a standard of care for mediators.

STANDARD I. SELF-DETERMINATION

A. A mediator shall conduct a mediation based on the principle of party self-determination. Self-determination is the act of coming to a voluntary, uncoerced decision in which each party makes free and informed choices as to process and outcome. Parties may exercise self-determination at any stage of a mediation, including mediator selection, process design, participation in or withdrawal from the process, and outcomes.
   1. Although party self-determination for process design is a fundamental principle of mediation practice, a mediator may need to balance such party self-determination with a mediator's duty to conduct a quality process in accordance with these Standards.
   2. A mediator cannot personally ensure that each party has made free and informed choices to reach particular decisions, but, where appropriate, a mediator should make the parties aware of the importance of consulting other professionals to help them make informed choices.
B. A mediator shall not undermine party self-determination by any party for reasons such as higher settlement rates, egos, increased fees, or outside pressures from court personnel, program administrators, provider organizations, the media or others.

STANDARD II. IMPARTIALITY

A. A mediator shall decline a mediation if the mediator cannot conduct it in an impartial manner. Impartiality means freedom from favoritism, bias or prejudice.
B. A mediator shall conduct a mediation in an impartial manner and avoid conduct that gives the appearance of partiality.
   1. A mediator should not act with partiality or prejudice based on any participant's personal characteristics, background, values and beliefs, or performance at a mediation, or any other reason.
   2. A mediator should neither give nor accept a gift, favor, loan or other item of value that raises a question as to the mediator's actual or perceived impartiality.
   3. A mediator may accept or give de minimis gifts or incidental items or services that are provided to facilitate a mediation or respect cultural norms so long as

such practices do not raise questions as to a mediator's actual or perceived impartiality.

C. If at any time a mediator is unable to conduct a mediation in an impartial manner, the mediator shall withdraw.

STANDARD III. CONFLICTS OF INTEREST

A. A mediator shall avoid a conflict of interest or the appearance of a conflict of interest during and after a mediation. A conflict of interest can arise from involvement by a mediator with the subject matter of the dispute or from any relationship between a mediator and any mediation participant, whether past or present, personal or professional, that reasonably raises a question of a mediator's impartiality.

B. A mediator shall make a reasonable inquiry to determine whether there are any facts that a reasonable individual would consider likely to create a potential or actual conflict of interest for a mediator. A mediator's actions necessary to accomplish a reasonable inquiry into potential conflicts of interest may vary based on practice context.

C. A mediator shall disclose, as soon as practicable, all actual and potential conflicts of interest that are reasonably known to the mediator and could reasonably be seen as raising a question about the mediator's impartiality. After disclosure, if all parties agree, the mediator may proceed with the mediation.

D. If a mediator learns any fact after accepting a mediation that raises a question with respect to that mediator's service creating a potential or actual conflict of interest, the mediator shall disclose it as quickly as practicable. After disclosure, if all parties agree, the mediator may proceed with the mediation.

E. If a mediator's conflict of interest might reasonably be viewed as undermining the integrity of the mediation, a mediator shall withdraw from or decline to proceed with the mediation regardless of the expressed desire or agreement of the parties to the contrary.

F. Subsequent to a mediation, a mediator shall not establish another relationship with any of the participants in any matter that would raise questions about the integrity of the mediation. When a mediator develops personal or professional relationships with parties, other individuals or organizations following a mediation in which they were involved, the mediator should consider factors such as time elapsed following the mediation, the nature of the relationships established, and services offered when determining whether the relationships might create a perceived or actual conflict of interest.

STANDARD IV. COMPETENCE

A. A mediator shall mediate only when the mediator has the necessary competence to satisfy the reasonable expectations of the parties.

1. Any person may be selected as a mediator, provided that the parties are satisfied with the mediator's competence and qualifications. Training, experience in mediation, skills, cultural understandings and other qualities are often necessary for mediator competence. A person who offers to serve as a mediator creates the expectation that the person is competent to mediate effectively.
2. A mediator should attend educational programs and related activities to maintain and enhance the mediator's knowledge and skills related to mediation.
3. A mediator should have available for the parties' information relevant to the mediator's training, education, experience and approach to conducting a mediation.

B. If a mediator, during the course of a mediation determines that the mediator cannot conduct the mediation competently, the mediator shall discuss that determination with the parties as soon as is practicable and take appropriate steps to address the situation, including, but not limited to, withdrawing or requesting appropriate assistance.

C. If a mediator's ability to conduct a mediation is impaired by drugs, alcohol, medication or otherwise, the mediator shall not conduct the mediation.

STANDARD V. CONFIDENTIALITY

A. A mediator shall maintain the confidentiality of all information obtained by the mediator in mediation, unless otherwise agreed to by the parties or required by applicable law.

1. If the parties to a mediation agree that the mediator may disclose information obtained during the mediation, the mediator may do so.
2. A mediator should not communicate to any non-participant information about how the parties acted in the mediation. A mediator may report, if required, whether parties appeared at a scheduled mediation and whether or not the parties reached a resolution.
3. If a mediator participates in teaching, research or evaluation of mediation, the mediator should protect the anonymity of the parties and abide by their reasonable expectations regarding confidentiality.

B. A mediator who meets with any persons in private session during a mediation shall not convey directly or indirectly to any other person, any information that was obtained during that private session without the consent of the disclosing person.

C. A mediator shall promote understanding among the parties of the extent to which the parties will maintain confidentiality of information they obtain in a mediation.

D. Depending on the circumstance of a mediation, the parties may have varying expectations regarding confidentiality that a mediator should address. The parties may make their own rules with respect to confidentiality, or the accepted practice of an individual mediator or institution may dictate a particular set of expectations.

STANDARD VI.   QUALITY OF THE PROCESS

A. A mediator shall conduct a mediation in accordance with these Standards and in a manner that promotes diligence, timeliness, safety, presence of the appropriate participants, party participation, procedural fairness, party competency and mutual respect among all participants.

   1. A mediator should agree to mediate only when the mediator is prepared to commit the attention essential to an effective mediation.
   2. A mediator should only accept cases when the mediator can satisfy the reasonable expectation of the parties concerning the timing of a mediation.
   3. The presence or absence of persons at a mediation depends on the agreement of the parties and the mediator. The parties and mediator may agree that others may be excluded from particular sessions or from all sessions.
   4. A mediator should promote honesty and candor between and among all participants, and a mediator shall not knowingly misrepresent any material fact or circumstance in the course of a mediation.
   5. The role of a mediator differs substantially from other professional roles. Mixing the role of a mediator and the role of another profession is problematic and thus, a mediator should distinguish between the roles. A mediator may provide information that the mediator is qualified by training or experience to provide, only if the mediator can do so consistent with these Standards.
   6. A mediator shall not conduct a dispute resolution procedure other than mediation but label it mediation in an effort to gain the protection of rules, statutes, or other governing authorities pertaining to mediation.
   7. A mediator may recommend, when appropriate, that parties consider resolving their dispute through arbitration, counseling, neutral evaluation or other processes.
   8. A mediator shall not undertake an additional dispute resolution role in the same matter without the consent of the parties. Before providing such service, a mediator shall inform the parties of the implications of the change in process and ob-

Model Standards of Conduct for Mediators

tain their consent to the change. A mediator who undertakes such role assumes different duties and responsibilities that may be governed by other standards.

9. If a mediation is being used to further criminal conduct, a mediator should take appropriate steps including, if necessary, postponing, withdrawing from or terminating the mediation.

10. If a party appears to have difficulty comprehending the process, issues, or settlement options, or difficulty participating in a mediation, the mediator should explore the circumstances and potential accommodations, modifications or adjustments that would make possible the party's capacity to comprehend, participate and exercise self-determination.

B. If a mediator is made aware of domestic abuse or violence among the parties, the mediator shall take appropriate steps including, if necessary, postponing, withdrawing from or terminating the mediation.

C. If a mediator believes that participant conduct, including that of the mediator, jeopardizes conducting a mediation consistent with these Standards, a mediator shall take appropriate steps including, if necessary, postponing, withdrawing from or terminating the mediation.

STANDARD VII.   ADVERTISING AND SOLICITATION

A. A mediator shall be truthful and not misleading when advertising, soliciting or otherwise communicating the mediator's qualifications, experience, services and fees.

1. A mediator should not include any promises as to outcome in communications, including business cards, stationery, or computer-based communications.

2. A mediator should only claim to meet the mediator qualifications of a governmental entity or private organization if that entity or organization has a recognized procedure for qualifying mediators and it grants such status to the mediator.

B. A mediator shall not solicit in a manner that gives an appearance of partiality for or against a party or otherwise undermines the integrity of the process.

C. A mediator shall not communicate to others, in promotional materials or through other forms of communication, the names of persons served without their permission.

STANDARD VIII.   FEES AND OTHER CHARGES

A. A mediator shall provide each party or each party's representative true and complete information about mediation fees, expenses and any other actual or potential charges that may be incurred in connection with a mediation.

1. If a mediator charges fees, the mediator should develop them in light of all relevant factors, including the type and complexity of the matter, the qualifications of the mediator, the time required and the rates customary for such mediation services.
2. A mediator's fee arrangement should be in writing unless the parties request otherwise.

B. A mediator shall not charge fees in a manner that impairs a mediator's impartiality.
1. A mediator should not enter into a fee agreement which is contingent upon the result of the mediation or amount of the settlement.
2. While a mediator may accept unequal fee payments from the parties, a mediator should not allow such a fee arrangement to adversely impact the mediator's ability to conduct a mediation in an impartial manner.

STANDARD IX.   ADVANCEMENT OF MEDIATION PRACTICE

A. A mediator should act in a manner that advances the practice of mediation. A mediator promotes this Standard by engaging in some or all of the following:
1. Fostering diversity within the field of mediation.
2. Striving to make mediation accessible to those who elect to use it, including providing services at a reduced rate or on a pro bono basis as appropriate.
3. Participating in research when given the opportunity, including obtaining participant feedback when appropriate.
4. Participating in outreach and education efforts to assist the public in developing an improved understanding of, and appreciation for, mediation.
5. Assisting newer mediators through training, mentoring and networking.

B. A mediator should demonstrate respect for differing points of view within the field, seek to learn from other mediators and work together with other mediators to improve the profession and better serve people in conflict.

Copyright © 2005 by the American Bar Association. Reprinted with permission. This information or any or portion thereof may not be copied or disseminated in any form or by any means or stored in an electronic database or retrieval system without the express written consent of the American Bar Association.

Appendix F

Sample Rules of Mediation

ALTHOUGH DIFFERENT mediation services have their own sets of rules, what you see below is a typical example of what you might encounter as a mediator. The following rules are used by the Center for Conflict Resolution at Brigham Young University.

1. GOOD FAITH EFFORT

Parties in the mediation process agree to make a good faith effort to resolve their conflict, which means to make an honest endeavor to participate in communications or conferences with the other party with the purpose of reaching a mutually acceptable settlement.

2. CONFIDENTIALITY

Except as otherwise agreed by the parties or permitted by law, any oral or written communications prepared specifically for or expressed in the course of the mediation proceeding are privileged and confidential and shall not be disclosed through discovery or any other compulsory process and are not admissible as evidence in any judicial or arbitration proceeding. Audio or visual recordings of mediation communications, electronic or otherwise, are not permissible. Exceptions to the rule of confidentiality in mediation communications that are permitted by law involve immediate threats of physical violence or when child abuse is suspected or reported. Any documents that are produced as a result of mediation, such as a settlement agreement or summary of decisions reached, may be used by participants in subsequent relevant proceedings.

3. COURTESY

The parties agree to be courteous throughout the mediation process by respecting the opinions, perceptions, and feelings of the other parties and by refraining from personal attacks, intimidation, threats, and verbal or physical abuse.

4. ROLE OF THE MEDIATOR

The mediator may conduct joint and separate meetings with the parties and may suggest resolutions to the conflict, but does not have authority to impose a settlement.

5. REPRESENTATION

Any party to the mediation may be represented by another person provided that the representative has sufficient knowledge of the problem and full authority to make and sign a binding agreement on behalf of the represented party, and that efforts to mediate with the representative are likely to enhance the possibility of achieving a settlement

6. LEGAL COUNSEL

The parties may consult legal counsel any time during the mediation process. The mediator has no duty to protect the interests of the parties or to provide them with information about their legal rights.

7. TERMINATION OF MEDIATION

The mediation process is terminated when (a) the parties reach a settlement agreement; (b) the mediator determines that further efforts at mediation are no longer likely to achieve a settlement; (c) both parties withdraw from the mediation proceedings; or (d) the BYU Center for Conflict Resolution declares that a party may bypass the mediation process and proceed to arbitration.

8. ARBITRATION AND COURT

Should the parties fail to settle their conflict, both parties, if eligible, may apply for binding arbitration with the BYU Center for Conflict Resolution; otherwise, legal remedies may be sought through the civil courts. The parties applying for arbitration must submit a written Demand or Submission Agreement for arbitration with the BYU Center for Conflict Resolution within 90 days after termination of the mediation.

9. EXCLUSION OF LIABILITY

Neither the university nor any mediator shall be liable to any party for any act or omission in connection with any mediation service or activity sponsored by the BYU Center for Conflict Resolution.

NOTES

NOTES

NOTES

NOTES

NOTES

NOTES

NOTES

NOTES

NOTES

NOTES